Dear Caroline,

Enjoy these macaws — as apparently as 4 year old childhood...

Love Ruth x

ENCYCLOPEDIA OF MACAWS

WERNER LANTERMANN

Translated by WILLIAM CHARLTON

Photographs: Olaf Amme; Anthony Verlag: Keseberg; Thomas Arndt; Glen S. Axelrod; Herbert R. Axelrod; Heiko Bleher; Thomas Brosset; Dr. E. W. Burr; Rod Cathcart; Alan R. Christian; John Daniel; Michael DeFreitas; Sam Fehrenz; Isabelle Francais; Freizeitland Geiselwind; Steffen P. Goldhammer; W. R. Grace & Co.; Fred Hanson; Fred Harris; Dieter Hoppe; Ralph Kaehler; Dr. Klaus König; P. Leysen; Klaus-Peter Linn; Don Mathews; Max Meier; Berthold Meister; A. J. Mobbs; Dr. John Moore; Mosig-Käfigbau; Dr. E. J. Mulawka; Claus Nielsen; Aaron Norman; Paradise Park, Hawaii; Robert Pearcy; Robert Prange; Jürgen Preis; Dr. Paul Roth; San Diego Zoo; Dr. U. Schürer; Patrick Tay; Carol Thiem; Dale Thompson; Tony Tilford; Guy van den Bossche; Louise Van der Meid; Vogelpark Walsrode: Horst Müller, Klaus Trogisch; Don Wells; Roland Wirth. Drawings by Jürgen Ritter.

Title page: Hyacinth and Red-and-green macaws, photograph by Robert Pearcy.

Contents

In their homeland, hand-reared macaws are popular "playmates" for Indian children.

Foreword

Long before they were known in Europe, macaws were popular house pets of the Indians of the New World, whose liking for these impressive tropical birds rested on the animals' intelligence, mimicking ability, and quickly achieved tameness. Beyond that, the birds' colorful feathers were used as decoration.

The first macaws apparently reached Central Europe at the start of the seventeenth century, where they were in great demand, a circumstance which has not changed to the present day. For many people, including those who do not concern themselves with animals, macaws are the embodiment of the word "parrot."

In addition to the brilliantly colored large macaws, which as a rule are also recognized and addressed as such by the layman, this book also concerns itself with the less familiar species of the genus *Ara* as well as the rare blue macaws of the genera *Anodorhynchus* and *Cyanopsitta*.

This book was written first and foremost for the practitioner, be he fancier, breeder, or zoo keeper; beyond that, however, also for the ornithologist, who will obtain up-to-date information for his scientific work.

The inclusion of all living species would certainly have been impossible without the assistance of the following fanciers, keepers, and

Of the large blue macaws, in captivity the Blue-and-yellow (*Ara ararauna*) is the most common.

scientists, who readily provided information on questions of detail. All of them are given my heartfelt thanks: J. Bordiek, Vogelpark Metelen; Dr. R. Burkard, Baar, Switzerland; Prof. Dr. E. Curio, Ruhr-Universität, Bochum; Dr. A. E. Decoteau, Dunstable, United States; Dipl.-Biol. F. Ostenrath, Zoo Duisburg; Dipl.-Biol. R. Reinhard, Zoo Berlin; Dr. U. Schürer, Zoo Wuppertal; Prof. Dr. H. Sick, Academia Brasileira De Ciencias, Brazil; Dr. J. Steinbacher, Senckenbergmuseum, Frankfurt; E. Stirnberg, Tierpark, Bochum; Dr. D. Vogt, Zoo Krefeld.

The publication of *Aras* in its original edition (first printing, 1984) was due to the initiative of the publisher, Mr. H. Müller, Bomlitz.

WERNER LANTERMANN

Housed together, macaws of different species—such as the Red-and-green and Blue-and-yellow macaws here—are inclined to hybridize.

Introduction

"Many are the advantages that distinguish the bird from all other animals and even people. We envy it especially for the sake of its flight, the glorious gift, which bestows upon it a benevolent fate, of soaring up into the ether and floating high

the same relationship to us as the cockatoos, since neither can be considered as house pets, but rather can only be looked upon as ornamental birds for the antechamber, veranda, garden, or even for the poultry yard and park. As such, however, they also have a very special value in that they generally prove to be extremely

Splendid coloration and large size conspire to make the sight of a macaw in flight memorable.

above all other living creatures . . .

"Macaws are of special interest to the readers of this book from the start inasmuch as they first of all belong to the familiar talking parrots, which have been known since times of old . . . and all of them without exception are able to talk. The majority, namely the largest of them, of course stand in

hardy and persistent and can be kept outdoors throughout the mild seasons of the year. For this reason they are also prized showpieces for zoos and nature installations of that kind . . .

"Their homeland is exclusively America, where they occur from northern Mexico to southern Brazil and Paraguay. . . . Their flight is rapid; in the largest species, however, ponderous. Their sideways-strutting gait on the ground is clumsy; by comparison they climb nimbly and skillfully in branches. All kinds of tree fruits and seeds, especially rock-hard palm nuts, which they shatter with their powerful bills, are their food. As sedentary birds, they fly very far to raid the natives' crops, and since they cause all too much damage, they are keenly hunted, for the sake of their beautiful feathers and their, I confess, not particularly tasty flesh as well. . . .

"Macaws learn to mimic many words and sometimes complete sentences with a loud, powerful, though usually inarticulate, voice; in general, they lag far behind Grey Parrots and amazon parrots, as well as behind Alexandrine Parakeets (which are more closely related to them), whereas they are otherwise quite gifted mentally. The smaller species, on the other hand, fall considerably short of the larger ones in both respects" (Russ, 1882).

These words, with which Dr. Karl Russ introduced the chapter "Macaws" in his book *Die sprechenden Papageien* a little more than one hundred years ago, are still quite accurate even today.

Just as in the ancient cultures of past centuries, today many people are still fascinated by these splendidly colored exotic birds, which enjoy great popularity on account of, among other things, their mimicking ability.

For the fancier in Germany, however, the outbreak in 1930 of a parrot disease, which was unknown until that time and also communicable to people, meant the temporary end to the importation of psittacids. In the year 1934, the federal government of that time enacted a strict import ban in consideration of this disease, which

The waddling gait of macaws on a flat surface makes them amusing performers of tricks in parrot shows.

Outdoor macaw exhibit in the Walsrode bird park. With their flight feathers trimmed, the birds are kept outdoors during the warm seasons.

received the name "psittacosis" on account of the apparent connection with imported parrots.

When the ban was lifted in the year 1964, after an effective treatment for psittacosis was developed and regulated, the importation of parakeets and parrots expanded to an unimaginable degree.

For a time, certain species were captured in large numbers in their homelands and exported to Europe, so that years ago some responsible countries already prohibited the exportation of all animal and plant species to avoid promoting the senseless exploitation of nature. The warnings of concerned conservationists and ecologists died away unheard; and even the efforts of scientists and politicians from around the world, who assembled for the first time in Washington D.C., in 1973 and ratified an

international agreement (known by the name "CITES") to assist in the protection of endangered animal and plant species, have not been able to achieve the desired effect so far.

It seems almost as if these efforts achieved closer to the opposite effect with the people responsible, for up to the end of the 1970s greater and greater numbers of parrots—among them many rare species—were put on the market by unscrupulous animal collectors and importers. Combined with the destruction of the birds' native living spaces (through the clearing of rainforests and so forth), these actions have brought many parrot species to the brink of extinction. Of the more than 320 species of the order of parrots (Psittaciformes), at present only three are not threatened. All other species have been listed since July 1, 1983, in

number of birds imported from the native countries.

The collaboration of private breeders—with the inclusion of zoos and bird parks—is certainly inevitable in the long run, especially since efforts should be directed towards the exchange of available animal material, which makes so much more sense than having to turn to new importations constantly.

Unfortunately, this development has started very late, so that it appears questionable whether private individuals and zoological institutions, who have suitable parrot stocks at their disposal, will still be able to succeed in building up healthy breeding stocks to ensure the preservation of species in captivity. Therefore, it appears to me that the specialization of

Appendices I and II of CITES.

Even today macaws, along with the African Grey Parrot and various amazon parrot species, still number among the most common parrots in captivity, and are kept by fanciers for the most diverse reasons. Although the overwhelming majority of the imported birds end up in small cages, where they barely survive as house pets, in recent years an increased tendency to keep these large parrots in pairs has been observed. Many dedicated fanciers have now recognized the necessity of breeding as a contribution to the preservation of species in captivity. As can be concluded from specialist literature, the propagation of large parrots in captivity has increased in recent years—probably in part as a result of the development of methods for definitive sex determination—although the number of captive-bred birds is still greatly disproportionate to the

breeders on a few species is inevitable. As a rule, this is the only way for most breeders to be able to keep several pairs of a species in the amount of space which they have available, so that the young can later be mated with unrelated birds. This sort of breeding for preservation demands a large measure of idealism from the participants, so that without question only those fanciers who are not ruled by profit-seeking motives are addressed here.

The main concerns of this book thus consist of familiarizing the serious fancier with the situation of the declining parrot fauna. It is hoped that this book will encourage the fancier to give up the single keeping of parrots and to undertake breeding attempts in cooperation with like-minded persons.

Range of the
recent macaw
species.

Geographic Distribution

Macaws are distributed over large areas of South and Central America, and, with amazon parrots, are the most familiar representatives of the family of the so-called true parrots (Psittacidae) found there. The Tropics of Cancer and Capricorn can be considered as the rough boundaries of their geographic distribution, although Illiger's Macaw (*Ara maracana*) as well the Glaucous Macaw (*Anodorhynchus glaucus*) are found south as far as the 35th degree of latitude (northern Argentina and northern Uruguay), while the Military Macaw (*Ara militaris*) occurs beyond the Tropic of Cancer in northern Mexico. The greatest diversity of species is found north and south of the Amazon near the equator.

There is no doubt that macaws formerly occurred on the islands of the West Indies. With the exception of the Cuban Macaw (*Ara tricolor*), the existence of which is documented until the middle of the nineteenth century, several species died out there in the fifteenth and sixteenth centuries. Even before the discovery of these islands by Europeans, the populations of macaws that lived there had been decimated by the natives, who hunted the birds for food, as well as by annual hurricanes, which caused great damage to the living populations as well as the nesting and food trees.

Habitat of the Hyacinth Macaw (*Anodorhynchus hyacinthinus*) in the interior of Bahia, northeastern Brazil.

A Blue-and-yellow Macaw (*Ara ararauna*) in a setting not unlike that of its native environment.

Living Spaces of Macaws

In the huge area of distribution of the macaw species are found the most diverse climates and vegetational forms. The overwhelming majority of macaw species is concentrated in the rainforests and tropical savannas of the tropics. In addition, various

provides a permanently high level of humidity. The plants, which flourish here in an immense diversity of species, are not subject to periods of dormancy and bear fruit throughout the entire year.

The climate of the moist savannas resembles that of the tropical rainforest during most of the year. However, two rainless periods lasting a total of two to five months interrupt the annual rhythm. The temperature can vary up to 25° C

The three most familiar *Ara* macaws in captivity—the Scarlet, the Blue-and-yellow, and the Red-and-green—are also found in the same areas of tropical South America.

species have adapted to the dry and thornbush savannas as well as the riparian landscapes and forests of the subtropical zones.

A constant high temperature of an average of 28 to 30° C, which drops very little even at night, prevails in the rainforest. The amount of precipitation remains relatively constant throughout the year and

between day and night. The vegetation consists of tall clumps of hardy grasses and deciduous mixed forests.

Dry savannas are found on both sides of the equator in the regions of the Tropics of Cancer and Capricorn. Characteristic of these regions are the five to seven dry months, which are clearly

In the wild, members of a Scarlet Macaw (*Ara macao*) pair will stay close together.

detrimental to the growth of vegetation. Fields of low grasses, interspersed with isolated groups of trees and shrubs, form the plant cover. More than seven dry months allow only few plants to grow in the thornbush savannas. The sparse grass cover is only occasionally broken up by widely spaced dry forests, thorn bushes, and cacti. The average annual temperature is seldom lower than 20° C.

The subtropical zones beyond the Tropics of Capricorn and Cancer are characterized by warm, rainy summers and moderately warm, rainless winters. They represent the zone of transition between the tropics and the temperate zones.

Left: In the Red-shouldered Macaw, the subspecies *Ara nobilis cumanensis* differs from the nominate form principally by its light upper mandible.

Below: Recently fledged Blue-and-yellow Macaws (*Ara ararauna*) at twelve weeks of age. The dark eye color is the main feature that distinguishes them from adults.

Systematic Position

Parrots form a self-contained group sharply set off from other bird groups, which are united in the order Psittaciformes. On the basis of anatomic homologies, systematists as a rule classify them close to the "yoke-toed" (zygodactylous) birds, such as cuckoos, woodpeckers, and so forth, which—like parrots—always exhibit two toes in front and two behind.

Von Boetticher (1964), however, entertains doubts about this taxonomic classification. He believes that the evolution of the yoke-toed foot could have been the result of parallel adaptation to similar living conditions, so that it could have evolved independently in different groups and need not indicate necessarily a close phylogenetic relationship.

In the classification by Peters (1937), the parrots are placed after the pigeons and before the touracos, cuckoos, and owls. The great uniformity of forms makes the classification of the order Psittaciformes more difficult.

Peters (1937), Brereton and Immelmann (1962), Von Boetticher (1964), among others, propose

Facing page: A group of *Ara* macaws on display in a shop.

Below: "Collecting center" of a South American importer, who packs the captured parrots together in the smallest possible space before they are sold. For perching only plain metal rods are available. Conures and amazon parrots keep company with Chestnut-fronted and Red-fronted macaws.

In the Chestnut-fronted Macaw (*Ara severa*), two subspecies are distinguished on the basis of size.

different taxonomic classifications, which will not be discussed in more detail here. The more recent works of Forshaw (1973) and Wolters (1975) are the basis for this representation.

Forshaw (1973) divides the order into three families, which in turn are divided into subfamilies. The three macaw genera *Cyanopsitta*, *Anodorhynchus*, and *Ara* are classified in the subfamily Psittacinae of the parrot family Psittacidae. Within these genera he recognizes, in addition to the monotypic genus *Cyanopsitta*, three

species in *Anodorhynchus* and 15 species, including two extinct forms, in *Ara*.

Wolters (1975) adopts a considerably more detailed view. He divides the order Psittaciformes into 11 families. Macaws are placed—classified in four genera—in the subfamily Aratinginae within the family Psittacidae (true parrots). Wolters also recognizes one species in the genus *Cyanopsitta* and three species in *Anodorhynchus*. Within the genus *Ara*, however, he recognizes—in contrast to Forshaw (1973)—only 12 living species. In his interpretation, the smallest species, the Red-shouldered Macaw, with the nominate form *Diopsittaca nobilis* and the subspecies *D. n. cumensis* = *hahni*, is the only species in the genus *Diopsittaca* (Linné, 1758).

To provide a better overview, the English and scientific names of all living species and subspecies of the three macaw genera are listed below. The order of presentation corresponds to that of Forshaw (1973), although the extinct species he lists are not mentioned.

The designation Caninde Macaw (*Ara candinde*), which has been in use through the present, was changed on the basis of recent scientific research. The new, more correct, designation is the Blue-throated Macaw (*Ara glaucogularis*).

Genus: *Anodorhynchus*
— *hyacinthinus*   Hyacinth Macaw
— *glaucus*   Glaucous Macaw
— *leari*   Lear's Macaw

Genus: *Cyanopsitta*

— *spixii*   Spix's Macaw

Genus: *Ara*

— *ararauna*	Blue-and-yellow Macaw
— *glaucogularis*	Blue-throated Macaw (formerly Caninde Macaw)
— *militaris*	Military Macaw
— *m. militaris*	
— *m. mexicana*	
— *m. boliviana*	
— *ambigua*	Great Green Macaw
— *a. ambigua*	
— *a. guayaquilensis*	
— *macao*	Scarlet Macaw
— *chloroptera*	Red-and-green Macaw
— *rubrogenys*	Red-fronted Macaw
— *auricollis*	Yellow-collared Macaw
— *severa*	Chestnut-fronted Macaw
— *s. severa*	
— *s. castaneifrons*	
— *manilata*	Red-bellied Macaw
— *maracana*	Illiger's Macaw
— *couloni*	Blue-headed Macaw
— *nobilis*	Red-shouldered Macaw
— *n. nobilis*	
— *n. cumanensis*	
— *n. longipennis*	

Members of the genus *Ara*, like the Blue-and-yellow Macaw, are characterized by the mostly bare facial patches and a long, gradated tail.

Diagram A: Systematic Placement of the Macaw Genera According to Forshaw (1973)

(The extinct species mentioned by Forshaw are not included.)

ORDER

PARROTS

FAMILIES

| Loriidae | PSITTACIDAE | Cacatuidae |

SUBFAMILIES

| Micropsittinae | PSITTACINAE | Strigopinae | Nestorinae |

GENERA

Opopsitta	Psittrichas	Cyanoramphus	Poicephalus	Cyanoliseus	Pionites
Psittaculirostris	Prosopeia	Eunymphicus	Agapornis	Phyrrhura	Pionopsitta
Bolbopsittacus	Alisterus	Neophema	Loriculus	Enicognatus	Gypossitta
Psittinus	Aprosmictus	Lathamus	Psittacula	Myiopsitta	Hapalopsittaca
Psittacella	Polytelis	Melopsittacus	Aratinga	Bolborhynchus	Graydidascalus
Geoffroyus	Purpureicephalus	Pezoporus	Nandayus	Forpus	Pionus
Prioniturus	Barnardius	Geopsittacus	Leptosittaca	Brotogeris	Amazona
Tanygnathus	Platycercus	Coracopsis	Ognorhynchus	Nannopsittaca	Derotypus
Eclectus	Psephotus	Psittacus	Rhynchopsitta	Touit	Triclaria

| *ANODORHYNCHUS* | *CYANOPSITTA* | *ARA* |

SPECIES

1. *A. hyacinthinus* (Hyacinth Macaw)
2. *A. glaucus* (Glaucous Macaw)
3. *A. leari* (Lear's Macaw)

SPECIES

1. *C. spixii* (Spix's Macaw)

SPECIES

1. *A. ararauna* (Blue-and-yellow Macaw)
2. *A. glaucogularis* (Blue-throated Macaw)
3. *A. militaris* (Military Macaw)
4. *A. ambigua* (Great Green Macaw)
5. *A. macao* (Scarlet Macaw)
6. *A. chloroptera* (Red-and-green Macaw)
7. *A. rubrogenys* (Red-fronted Macaw)
8. *A. auricollis* (Yellow-collared Macaw)
9. *A. severa* (Chestnut-fronted Macaw)
10. *A. manilata* (Red-bellied Macaw)
11. *A. maracana* (Illiger's Macaw)
12. *A. couloni* (Blue-headed Macaw)
13. *A. nobilis* (Red-shouldered Macaw)

Diagram B: Systematic Placement of the Macaw Genera According to Wolters (1975)

(The extinct species mentioned by Wolters are not included.)

ORDER

Parrots
(Psittaciformes)

FAMILIES

Small Parrots
(Micropsittidae)

True Parrots
(Psittacidae)

Noble Parrots
(Psittaculidae)

Splendid Parakeets
(Polytelidae)

Lories
(Loriidae)

Broad-tailed Parakeets
(Platycercidae)

Budgerigars
(Melopsittacidae)

Ground Parakeets
(Pezoporidae)

Owl Parrots
(Strigopidae)

Cockatoos
(Cacatuidae)

Nestor Parrots
(Nestoridae)

SUBFAMILIES

Sparrow Parrots
(Forpinae)

Wedge-tailed
Parakeets (Aratinginae)

Small-billed Parakeets
(Brotogeryinae)

Amazon Parrots
(Amazoninae)

Parakeet Parrots
(Triclariinae)

White-bellied Parrots
(Pionitinae)

Grey Parrots
(Psittacinae)

Raven Parrots
(Coracopinae)

GENERA

Anodorhynchus

Cyanopsitta

Ara

Diopsittaca

Thectocercus

Guaruba

Nandayus

Rhynchopsitta

Psittacara

Aratinga

Eupsittula

Conuropsis

Ognorhynchus

Leptosittaca

Pyrrhura

Enicognathus

Cyanoliseus

Myiopsitta

SPECIES

Anodorhynchus

Hyacinth Macaw
(A. hyacinthinus)

Glaucous Macaw
(A. glaucus)

Lear's Macaw
(A. leari)

Cyanopsitta

Spix's Macaw
(C. spixii)

Ara

Caninde Macaw
(A. caninde)

Blue-and-yellow Macaw
(A. ararauna)

Red-fronted Macaw
(A. rubrogenys)

Chestnut-fronted Macaw
(A. severa)

Yellow-collared Macaw
(A. auricollis)

Blue-headed Macaw
(A. couloni)

Illiger's Macaw
(A. maracana)

Red-bellied Macaw
(A. manilata)

Military Macaw
(A. militaris)

Great Green Macaw
(A. ambigua)

Red-and-Green Macaw
(A. chloroptera)

Scarlet Macaw
(A. macao)

Diopsittaca

Red-shouldered Macaw
(D. nobilis)

Above: A particularly robust specimen of the Great Green Macaw (*Ara ambigua*), next to which a Blue-and-yellow Macaw (*Ara ararauna*) looks relatively small.

Right: Scarlet Macaw (*Ara macao*).

The Blue-throated Macaw (*Ara glaucogularis*), which up to now has commonly been called the Caninde Macaw, occupies a special position among the living representatives of the genus *Ara*. Besides the problem of the correct naming (see Ingels *et al*, 1981), the validity of this macaw form as an independent species or subspecies of *Ara ararauna* is also questioned.

Forshaw (1973) called this macaw a mysterious bird, the classification of which as a species, subspecies, or even as a juvenile form of the Blue-and-yellow Macaw is not clear.

In the meantime, the last supposition has been refuted. Captive breedings have shown that juvenile Blue-and-yellow Macaws differ from the adult form only in the color of the eyes.

Reinhard (1982) occupied himself with the still debatable question of the validity of this macaw as an independent species or a subspecies of the Blue-and-yellow Macaw. In addition to the differences in body size and coloration, he above all cites the different calls, a criterion of great importance in the systematic classification of phenotypically similar animals. Furthermore, he points out that both forms coexist in parts of their range without recognizable hybrids, which argues in favor of the presence of species and not of subspecies.

Wolters (1975) also seems to entertain some doubts about the systematic determination of this form; however, even though he provides it with a question mark, he considers it to be an independent species.

A paper by Ingels, Parkes, and Farrand (1981), in addition to dealing with the taxonomic validity, above all discusses the correct naming of this macaw form. Through the intensive study of the

24

older specialist literature, the authors determined that the specific name *caninde* is a synonym of *ararauna*, and therefore may not be used with this second blue-yellow macaw form. The specific name *glaucogularis*, which was first used by Dabenne (1921), must be used in place of *caninde* in the future.

The validity of this macaw form is less debatable to the authors. They consider it—just as does Wolters—to be an independent species, yet closely related to *ararauna*.

Left: The Scarlet Macaw (*Ara macao*) has also been called the Red-blue-and-yellow Macaw. *Below:* A Blue-and-yellow Macaw (*Ara ararauna*) with wings heavily clipped for training.

Of the well-known large macaws, the Scarlet (*Ara macao*) appears to be the most threatened species.

Species Threatened with Extinction

Because of increasing changes to their original living spaces—the continual spread of agricultural zones and increased cutting of forests—as well as unregulated collecting for zoos and parrot fanciers throughout the world, many parrot species are now on the brink of extinction.

For a number of years, an international commission has been concerned with the problems of flora and fauna threatened with extinction. An international agreement that regulates the capture and trade of threatened species has existed since 1973 under the name "CITES," and in the meantime has been ratified by many member nations. The Federal Republic of Germany signed this treaty in 1976, but so far it has not been able to enforce the agreement which it ratified on the importation of threatened species, so that as before

The large macaws are gregarious, and the mixed collections exhibited in zoos and bird parks provide abundant examples of friendly interaction between individuals.

certain species can be put on the market by unscrupulous importers.

Of the macaw species, besides the extremely rare Spix's Macaw (*Cyanopsitta spixii*), the small Glaucous and Lear's Macaws (*Anodorhynchus glaucus* and *Anodorhynchus leari*) face the greatest threat of extinction and are listed in Appendix I of CITES. All other species of macaws have been listed in Appendix II of this treaty since July 1, 1981. The fourth conference of CITES treaty members was held from April 19, 1983 to April 30, 1983 in Gaborone/Botswana. Effective from July 27, 1983, the Blue-throated Macaw (*Ara glaucogularis*) as well as the Red-fronted Macaw (*Ara rubrogenys*) are now also listed in Appendix I of CITES.

The scientific authority in the Federal Republic of Germany is the Bundesamt für Ernährung und Forstwirtschaft, Adickesallee 40, 6000 Frankfurt am Main 1, Postfach 18 02 03.

The regulation of imports by the agency of the legislators is intended to end the commercial trade in threatened animal and plant species. In special cases the import or export of threatened species is permitted if it has been guaranteed that this trade is not detrimental to the survival of the species and is not principally carried out for commercial purposes.

A variable distribution through a large range makes it difficult to assess the current status of the Chestnut-fronted Macaw (Ara severa).

Extinct Species

The former distribution of macaws on the islands of the West Indies (Bahamas, Greater and Lesser Antilles, Virgin Islands) is beyond question. With the exception of the Cuban Macaw (*Ara tricolor*), whose existence can be substantiated through several museum specimens, it is, however, extremely difficult to document the occurrence of the following described species. Travel reports and illustrations in old ship's logs must be relied on for this information. Any details on the external appearance of certain species are scarcely known; it is quite possible that they were identical with living species.

Genus: *Anodorhynchus*
a) *Anodorhynchus purpurascens*

This bird apparently was a large violet-blue macaw, which Rothschild (1907) classified in the genus *Anodorhynchus*. On its native island of Guadeloupe, it was hunted by the natives for its ornamental tail feathers and for food. It was already extinct when the first Europeans discovered Guadeloupe.

Genus: *Ara*
a) *Ara authocthones*

No details exist on the external appearance of this macaw, which formerly inhabited the island of St. Croix (Virgin Islands). The form is known only from fossil excavations (Forshaw 1973).

b) *Ara atwoodi*

This apparently was a green-colored species, which inhabited the island of Dominica. No details are known.

c) *Ara erythrocephala*

Green-and-yellow Macaw; former range: Jamaica.

d) *Ara erythrura*

Yellow-blue-colored species, which lived on one or more islands of the West Indies.

e) *Ara gossei*

In 1847, the naturalist Gosse named and described this macaw species, which was sighted in small numbers on the island of Jamaica. It was yellow on the forehead, crown, and nape area, while the remaining areas of the body were scarlet, and the wings were marked with blue.

f) *Ara guadeloupensis*

Various seafarers of the fifteenth and sixteenth centuries, among them Christopher Columbus, remarked on this macaw in their records. It occurred on the islands of Guadeloupe, Martinique, and possibly Dominica.

The Caribbean Indians hunted it for food, while the first Europeans prized it as a cage bird. The Guadeloupe Red Macaw resembled the Scarlet Macaw (*Ara macao*) in appearance; however, in contrast to that species, it exhibited an intense red-colored tail.

g) *Ara martinica*

Rothschild (1907) described and named this species, which apparently was found only on the island of Martinique and which resembled the Blue-and-yellow Macaw (*Ara ararauna*).

It is believed that Christopher Columbus brought along several specimens of the Orange-bellied Macaw when he returned to Spain, where they were exhibited to the public.

The illustration here—and those on following pages—were first published in 1907 in Lord Rothschild's *Extinct Birds.* The artist depended entirely on the descriptions and sketches of traveling naturalists, who recorded their observations in diaries. For all these species (with the exception of the Cuban Macaw, for which its former occurrence on the island of Cuba can be confirmed by museum specimens) there is no definitive information about their appearance and existence, so that the possibility of their being the same as living species cannot be excluded.

The extensive resemblance between the living *Anodorhynchus* species and the extinct form *Anodorhynchus purpurascens* depicted here cannot be missed. First described in 1838 by Navarette, it was named formally by Rothschild in 1905.

h) *Ara tricolor*

It is possible to obtain detailed information on the external appearance of the Cuban Macaw from the analysis of museum skins, which are found in several American and European institutions. A total of 14 skins exist, of which five are kept in museums in the United States and nine in Europe.

A description of this macaw species is quoted here; it is taken from the work by Luther (1970): "Length 45–50 centimeters; scarlet; crown yellowish red; nape yellow; rump and uppertail coverts light blue; wings purple blue; lesser wing coverts edged reddish brown; tail blue with red bases of feathers on upper parts, underside red; undertail coverts blue."

The Cuban Macaw did not become extinct until the last century, approximately between 1864 and 1885. Man's intervention, shooting for food and collecting for cage exhibits and pets, is the only known cause which could have contributed to the extinction of this species.

ISLANDS OF THE WEST INDIES

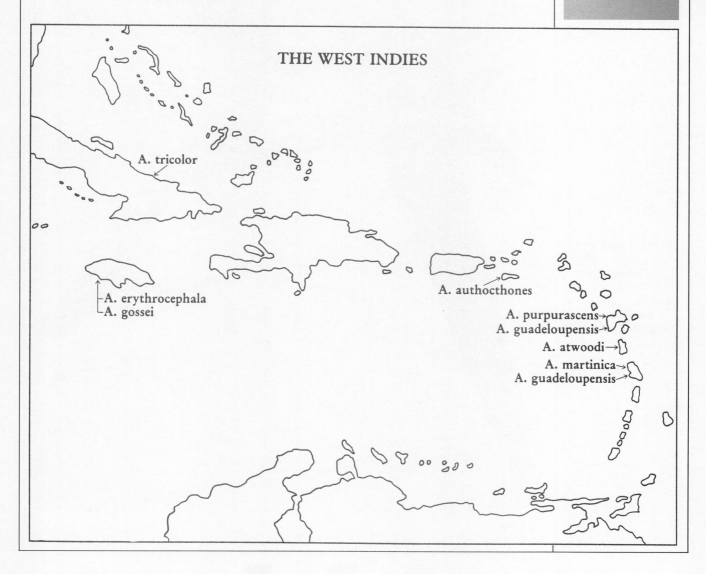

THE WEST INDIES

A. tricolor

A. erythrocephala
A. gossei

A. authocthones

A. purpurascens
A. guadeloupensis

A. atwoodi

A. martinica
A. guadeloupensis

The Green-and-yellow Macaw (*Ara erythrocephala*), which formerly occurred on the island of Jamaica, in part resembles the Great Green Macaw (*Ara ambigua*).

Facing page: The Mysterious Macaw (*Ara erythrura*), a blue-and-yellow-colored form, lived in the West Indies.

The Yellow-headed Macaw (*Ara gossei*), also called the Jamaican Macaw, was last seen in 1765 in the vicinity of the town of Lucea, in the northern part of the island. It is possible that *gossei* was an island form of the Cuban Macaw.

Apparently, the Orange-bellied Macaw (*Ara martinica*) occurred only on the island of Martinique.

The Cuban Macaw (*Ara tricolor*) was extirpated by the middle of the last century, it seems. Until 1885 there were reports of birds kept in captivity.

Anatomy and Physiology

Skeleton

The bird skeleton is characterized by its lightness, combined with great stability, which is achieved through the fusion of various parts of the skeleton. The light weight—for the special adaptation to a flying mode of life—is achieved through the development of thin-walled and air-filled hollow bones and a thin-shelled bone structure.

A conspicuous feature of all parrots is the robust, curved upper mandible, which is flexibly connected with the roundish oval cranial capsule. Together with the lower mandible, which—within certain limits—can be moved in all directions, there results an excellent instrument for picking up and breaking up food of all kinds. Additionally, the bill is of decisive physiological significance as a "third hand" in climbing.

The bill and claws are covered with horny tissue supplied with blood. This tissue grows continuously, which is counteracted by natural wear in the wild.

In captivity, a distorted relationship between growth and wearing can occasionally occur; in such cases, under certain circumstances small corrections may be necessary, whereby, however, a precise knowledge of the blood-conducting tissue is important.

On the inside of the upper mandible are found the so-called "rasplike grooves." These are horny indentations that make it easier to hold onto objects and to break up solid food into small pieces; these grooves also serve to sharpen and wear the lower mandible. Bill shape and size are directly related to body size as well as to the type of food eaten.

The feet of parrots have developed into climbing organs as an adaptation to their arboreal habits. The position of the toes—the first and fourth point to the rear, the second and third to the front—turns the parrot foot, like that of toucans and woodpeckers, into an ideal grasping and climbing tool, which together with the pronounced bill is very well adapted for a climbing manner of locomotion.

The wings are analogous to the forelegs of mammals. As a result of the development of a strong bony skeleton, the flying locomotion of the comparatively heavy parrots is made possible.

The rest of the skeleton consists of neck, breast, pelvic, and tail bones.

Musculature

Almost all birds exhibit strongly developed breast muscles, which are present in pairs. The smaller muscles lying underneath them act as antagonists to the breast muscles in the coordination of muscular strength necessary for all flight movements.

Also well developed are the muscles of the thigh and pelvic region, which transmit great strength to the legs and feet by means of long tendons. A special locking mechanism in the tendons that close the foot ensures that it

PARROT ANATOMY: THE SKELETON
(modified from Forshaw, 1973)

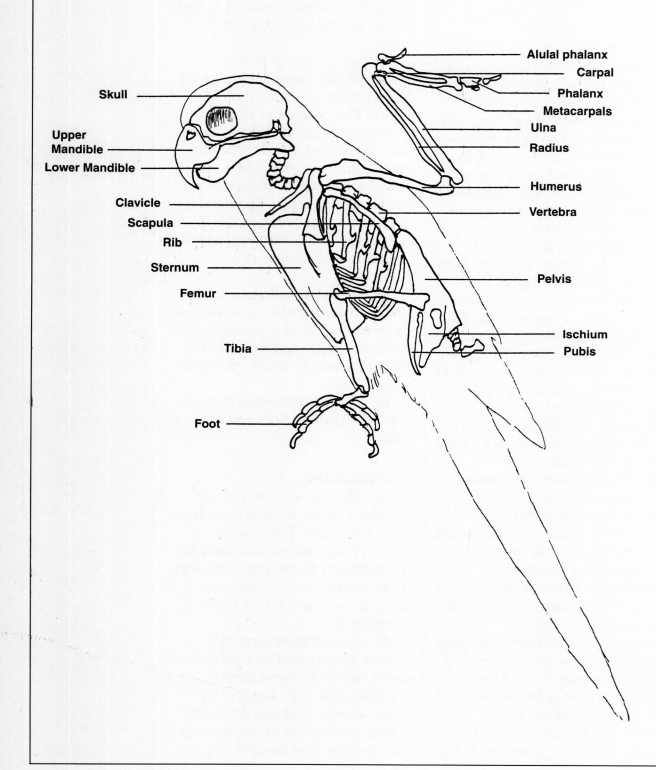

Skull

Upper Mandible

Lower Mandible

Clavicle

Scapula

Rib

Sternum

Femur

Tibia

Foot

Alulal phalanx

Carpal

Phalanx

Metacarpals

Ulna

Radius

Humerus

Vertebra

Pelvis

Ischium

Pubis

will remain closed without constant muscular tension while resting or sleeping.

The belly and back muscles are weak, while those of the neck and bill are extremely powerful. The great strength macaws can develop with their bills is thus easily explained.

Digestive organs

The tongue of the macaw is a muscular, fleshy organ, which by means of the gustatory nerves on the tip of the tongue permits the discrimination of edible and inedible food. Together with the upper and lower mandibles, it permits the breaking up and hulling of seeds.

Innumerable salivary glands in the oral cavity make it easier for solid food to pass on to the crop.

The gullet widens at its end into the crop, which stores and softens the food and later passes it on to the proventriculus.

Here the food is mixed with digestive juices (consisting of the enzymes pepsin, hydrochloric acid, and others), which are produced in the proventriculus, and is further predigested. In the same way as the crop, the proventriculus can also store food, which makes it possible for the bird to take up a fairly large amount of food when a surplus of suitable fruits or seeds is available at a feeding site.

After passing through the proventriculus, the food reaches the ventriculus, which consists of two pairs of muscles. The hard components of the food are ground between these muscles. Small stones that have been taken up intensify their grinding effect. If neither sand nor grit is available to birds in captivity for a fairly long time, their regular digestion is jeopardized.

The remaining parts of the digestive tract consist of the duodenum, small intestine, and rectum. In the rectum a portion of the water is removed from the droppings before they are excreted.

Plumage

The plumage of birds is in part an adaptation to their flying habits. Beyond that, in view of the high body temperature of birds, it performs an important role in heat insulation.

The feathers can be roughly divided into contour feathers and down feathers. They are made of a horny substance and consist of a quill and vanes. The primaries of the wings and the tail feathers are the largest contour feathers. Down is found in young birds as well as in the underflue of adult birds. Its only function is to prevent heat loss. In addition, many parrots possess so-called powder down, which continually discharge a powdery secretion which deposits itself on the outside of the contour feathers. The fatty dust has a similar effect to the oil of a preen gland. This has largely degenerated in parrots and has almost no function, so that— depending on the species—its original function is largely taken over by the powder down. The powder is water-repellent and protects the plumage against being soaked.

The coloration of the parrot's plumage results from the deposition of pigments as well as refractive

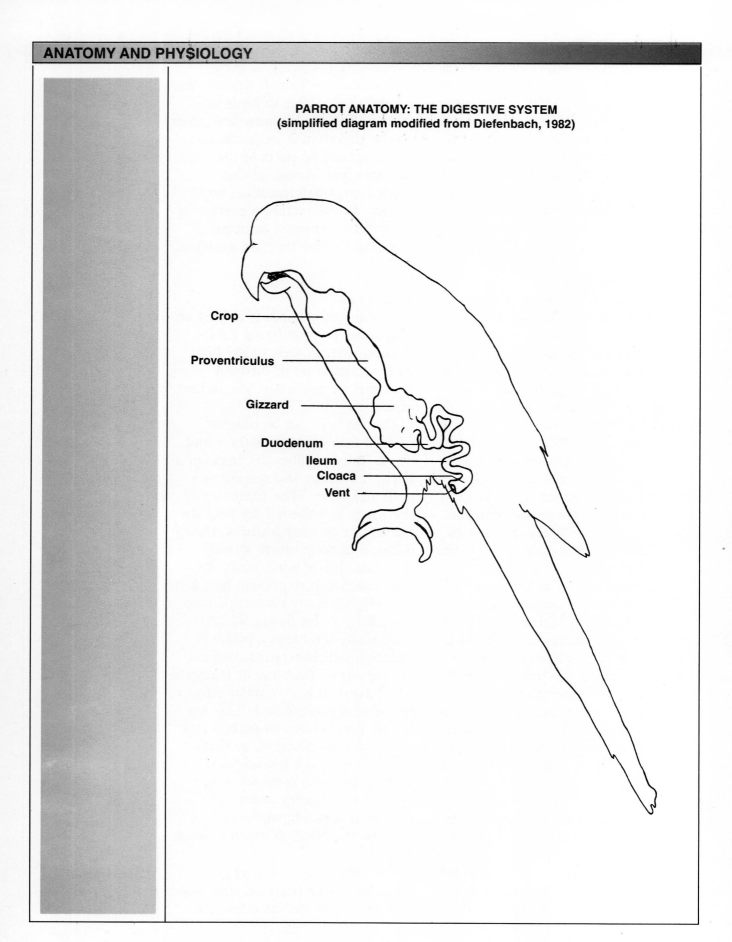

PARROT ANATOMY: THE DIGESTIVE SYSTEM
(simplified diagram modified from Diefenbach, 1982)

Crop

Proventriculus

Gizzard

Duodenum

Ileum

Cloaca

Vent

TOPOGRAPHIC DIAGRAM OF THE PLUMAGE

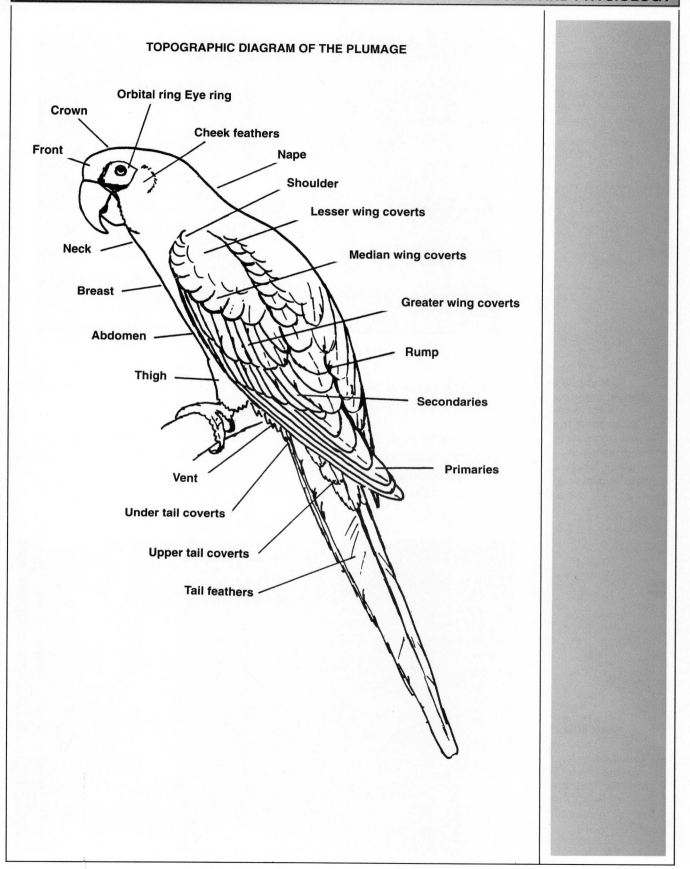

Orbital ring Eye ring

Crown

Cheek feathers

Front

Nape

Shoulder

Lesser wing coverts

Median wing coverts

Neck

Greater wing coverts

Breast

Abdomen

Rump

Thigh

Secondaries

Vent

Primaries

Under tail coverts

Upper tail coverts

Tail feathers

The trainer dispenses treats to the tame macaws at Parrot Jungle, Miami, Florida.

Facing page: Mutual preening serves to strengthen the pair bond, as in the Red-and-green Macaws (*Ara chloroptera*) here.

effects. The age and sex of a bird can have an effect on the intensity of the color.

The periodic molt found in many bird species is not characteristic of parrots. Parrots constantly renew shed feathers that are no longer functional, above all after breeding has been completed.

AUTHOR'S NOTE: *For the information on anatomy and physiology I am above all indebted to the works of Forshaw (1973), Pinter (1979), and Diefenbach (1982).*

As a hybrid macaw prepares to land on the trainer's arm, the feathers of the tail are spread.

Behavior

Observations of macaws in the wild are scarcely documented in literature. Besides diverse travel reports (Haverschmidt, 1968; Wetmore, 1968; Meyer de Schauensee, 1970; and others), which include various details on the habits of individual species, in Forshaw (1973) in particular there is a short summary of the biology and ethology of the three macaw genera.

The behavior of macaws in captivity—above all breeding behavior—has on the other hand been described by many authors (Risdon, 1965; Kirchhofer, 1973; Decoteau, 1982; Robiller and Trogisch, 1982; and many others). Deckert and Deckert (1982) as well as Hick (1962) concern themselves with the play behavior of individual species.

In the following section, elements of behavior frequently observed under captive conditions will be described. Studies of my own birds were supported by observations of Illiger's, Red-and-green, Military, and Hyacinth Macaws in the Bochum and Duisburg Zoos.

Nonsocial Behavior Patterns

Locomotion A climbing manner of locomotion—just as with many other parrots—is also observed to an increased degree with macaws and is supported by the zygodactyl-toe position as well as by the bill as an auxiliary grasping organ.

When walking on branches, one foot is placed in front of the other, whereby the bird turns the longitudinal axis of its body parallel to the direction of the branch. While walking and climbing principally serve for travelling short distances, larger distances are covered by flying. The flight of

large macaws, despite the stocky build, is agile, fast, and direct.

Some species, which as partial migrants move in response to the food supply present in a particular area, are persistent fliers able to travel distances of over 20 kilometers a day in flocks or small groups.

Facing page: **One Blue-and-yellow Macaw (*Ara ararauna*) solicits preening from another.**

Left: **The darkening of the normally medium-blue-colored wing and back plumage in this Blue-and-yellow Macaw (*Ara ararauna*) appears to be the result of a pigmentation disorder.**

Food intake In the wild, macaws feed on fruits, berries, buds, and a variety of seeds. During harvest time they often raid grain fields in fairly large numbers to feed on corn in different stages of ripeness. Often, the birds also cause great damage in banana plantations and are hunted relentlessly by the natives.

Seeds are hulled by pressing them with the tongue against the rasplike grooves in the upper mandible and then freeing them from the husk. Large seeds, pieces of fruit, and the like are held in the bill, then grasped by the foot, hulled or peeled, and eaten piece by piece. Great significance is attached to this behavior pattern in the taxonomic

classification of a bird species (refer to Smith, 1971).

Bathing In the species that have been studied so far, only bathing in water has been documented. Dust or sand baths, as are often encountered with other birds, have not been observed. Two basic types of bathing must be distinguished: bathing in containers and rain baths. Bathing in containers (or puddles) is often observed with females during the breeding season and apparently serves to regulate the humidity inside the nest cavity.

Macaws never stand with their feet in the water, but rather perch on the rim of the container. With ruffled plumage they plunge the head and front part of the body into the water in rapid succession and in this way wet those parts of the body that come into direct contact with the clutch during incubation.

This bathing behavior can also be observed occasionally outside the breeding season. Rain baths are clearly preferred, however. Such a bath begins with ruffled plumage and slightly drooping wings. In order to wet the plumage more thoroughly, later on this is accompanied by flapping of the wings and turning the body. At the same time, the tail feathers may be raised and spread.

Above: This melanistic Blue-and-yellow Macaw enjoys bathing in a washbasin.

In this view of a Scarlet Macaw (*Ara macao*) the coloration of the upper tail coverts is readily seen.

47

Right: When bathing in a container, macaws are loathe to step into the water and so perch on the edge.

Below: A view of the underwing coloration of a hybrid macaw.

Stretching movements Stretching movements are virtually identical in all macaw species. Both wings may be simultaneously spread slightly over the back or fully extended for a short time. Just as frequent is the stretching of one wing, which often follows right after the stretching movements. In this movement the wing's feathers are spread downward together with the foot and a part of the tail feathers on the same side of the body.

The simultaneous stretching of both wings has not been observed with macaws, although this behavior pattern is seen occasionally in other members of the family. Stretching movements occur throughout the day, but tend to follow a resting phase. The number of daily stretching movements varies, but clearly increases during the molt. In mated birds these movements are synchronous, an observation that was made by Dilger (1960) with *Agapornis* as well as by Diefenbach (1979) with *Cacatua*.

The "yawning" that is observed occasionally should probably be considered a stretching movement of the bill region. An increase in frequency, however, must be considered as a symptom of an illness of the respiratory tract, the bill cavity, the crop, or the like.

Scratching Simmons (1957) and Brereton and Immelmann (1962) point out the significance of

scratching behavior in the systematic classification of parrots. All macaw species scratch under the wings; that is, they lift the foot up to the head as when holding food and then perform scratching movements, usually in quick succession. If different areas of the head are to be scratched, the head is bowed down or otherwise put in a suitable position.

Bill care Like many other birds and parrots, macaws also clean their bills of adhering food by means of rubbing movements on a branch. If the food remains do not come loose even after repeated attempts, the bird brings a foot to the bill and attempts to clean it by using a movement similar to scratching.

Macaws spend a large part of the day gnawing the perches, whereby fresh wood is apparently preferred. This serves the natural wearing of the bill, as do the frequently heard "grating chewing sounds" while resting. These are produced by sharpening the lower mandible on the rasplike grooves of the upper mandible.

Preening refers to plumage grooming performed with the bill. In this fashion, breaks in the feather vanes are rejoined and feathers are repositioned. *Above*: The Military Macaw (*Ara militaris*); *below*: Blue-and-yellow Macaw (*Ara ararauna*).

Above: One macaw will often imitate the behavior of another: here two Red-and-green Macaws have their heads back, preening.

Right: Hyacinth Macaws (*Anodorhynchus hyacinthinus*). For macaws, the daily routine allows considerable time for resting and preening.

Resting and Sleeping All birds that have been observed spent a large part of the day resting. Observations in the wild have shown that the main phases of activity of macaws are in the early morning hours as well as in the afternoon and evening hours. The remainder of the time they perch with fluffed feathers and half-closed eyes in the top branches of a tree and rest. In so doing the head is occasionally turned over the back as in the sleeping position. The behavior of macaws in captivity does not differ from this description.

Sick adult birds and youngsters up to an age of five to six months, as a rule, rest on two legs; all other birds perch on one foot while resting or sleeping, while the other is tucked against the body and warmed in the plumage.

The sleeping position resembles the resting position. The bird closes its eyes completely and hides its head in its back plumage.

Social Behavior Highly evolved parrots, including macaws, live together in flocks outside the breeding season, which necessarily promotes the growth of social altercations. The individual sphere is limited in the flock and the delimitation of a territory is virtually impossible.

In the course of evolution, the increase in aggression that results from this must have been counteracted by a mechanism to limit aggression, which in certain situations made possible the suppression of the individual sphere.

Mating must be regarded as the extreme case here. In mating, on the one hand the tendency to take flight must be weakened and on the other the readiness to attack must be neutralized.

Captive macaws, such as this Blue-and-yellow (*Ara ararauna*), profit from the stimulation of outdoor sights and sounds.

Play Behavior Like all other highly evolved parrots, macaws—above all juveniles and subadult birds—are also distinguished by an unusual readiness to play. Deckert and Deckert (1982) differentiate between playful behavior and playing with objects (solitary play), as well as agonistic play (social play).

Besides playful behavior, which in the main does not consist of nonpractical fun climbing and flying movements, macaws also show great interest in playing with diverse objects. The Red-and-green Macaws described by Deckert and Deckert persistently occupied themselves with machine bolts, the nuts of which were not only unscrewed, but were also screwed on again with much effort. Hick (1962) observed a Hyacinth Macaw that liked to play with a ball.

The attraction of movable objects is also described by Teitler (1979), who trained her macaws—by using their own inclination to play—to pull small wheelbarrows and tricycles or to ride on roller skates. Furthermore, the described Hyacinth Macaw also took much pleasure in the most diverse sounds. It liked to drop objects that produced a loud sound to the floor, and then pick them up and drop them again.

Defense and fighting apparently play an important role in the life of adult macaws, so that parts of this behavior are tried out in play by subadult birds.

The natural playfulness of the large macaws, such as this Scarlet (*Ara macao*), disposes them to be adept at learning tricks.

Left: Macaws are featured performers in the show at Parrot Jungle in Florida.

Below: A group of Blue-and-yellow Macaws (*Ara ararauna*) in a holding cage.

Social Grooming Social grooming is of central importance within the social behavior of highly evolved birds. In addition to the benefits of the mutual cleaning of plumage in difficult-to-reach parts of the body (for example, in the head and rump areas), this behavior pattern above all serves to decrease aggression. It can be observed in birds of the same sex as well as in birds of different sexes and mated birds. The breeder can scarcely expect to gain any information for distinguishing the sexes from this, even though with heterosexually bonded birds this element occurs (negligibly) more often during courtship.

In the first encounter between two strange birds, within a short time mutual grooming can occur instead of aggressive behavior. In mated birds, social grooming has the effect of appeasing the mate as well as maintaining and strengthening the bond between the pair. In situations of conflict, it emphasizes the pair's feeling of belonging together and its readiness to defend its territory.

In the breeding season, particularly in the precopulative phase, the most important function of social grooming is as a "restraint to aggression." Only through the suppression of aggressive behavior patterns is the close approach and subsequent mating of two ready-to-breed birds made possible.

Facing page: Hyacinth Macaws (*Anodorhynchus hyacinthinus*) engaged in social grooming.

Above: A Blue-and- yellow (*Ara ararauna*) and a Scarlet Macaw (*A. macao*) preening one another.

Below: Mutual grooming is concentrated on the parts of the body the macaw cannot itself reach.

Reciprocal feeding—here performed by two Red-and-green Macaws (*Ara chloroptera*)—is a significant element of the pair-bonding process.

Facing page: Socialization between a Hyacinth (*Anodorhynchus hyacinthinus*) and a Red-and-green Macaw (*Ara chloroptera*).

Courtship Feeding In sexually mature, mated macaws, the element of courtship feeding is frequently observed. As a rule the cock feeds the hen: through bobbing head movements, the cock regurgitates food from its crop and gives it to the female; meanwhile, the hen assumes a posture similar to that of a dependent youngster and in so doing expresses appeasement, submission, and the readiness to mate.

In the same way as social grooming, courtship feeding also serves to maintain the pair bond; occasionally it can even be observed outside the breeding season with mated birds.

During breeding season this behavior pattern assumes another important function: it provides food to the incubating female, which during incubation and the first few days after the young hatch leaves the nest cavity only to defecate. If the cock fails as the provider during this time—because of injury, death, or the like—under certain circumstances the female can still rear the young alone.

Diefenbach (1979) observed in cockatoos of the genera *Callocephalon, Eolophus,* and *Cacatua* that because of alternating incubation by both sexes, the mutual provision of food does not occur and that consequently courtship feeding also did not occur during incubation or as an element of courtship.

Reproduction

The appearance of the breeding drive can counter flocking behavior in the wild. Two birds that are ready to mate separate from the flock and search for a nest cavity, which they often use many years in succession, in the tops of the rainforest giants. Preferred are nesting facilities at great height with an entrance hole as small as possible. Not until after the young are able to fly, which can often take three to four months, do the parents leave this breeding territory in order

Right: Yellow-collared Macaws (*Ara auricollis*).

For nesting, Blue-and-yellow Macaws (*Ara ararauna*) owned by H. Linn accepted a structure made of rough boards.

to join up with a flock again.

Observations in captivity suggest that all highly evolved species of parrots are monogamous for life, unless one bird dies prematurely or for some reason is no longer able to reproduce. Less highly evolved forms such as the Kakapo (*Strigops habroptilus*), the only species in the genus of the owl parrots (*Psittacidae*, *Strigopinae*), display only limited elements of social behavior. The cocks of this species live independently the whole year in the inaccessible mountains of New Zealand and only go in search of a mate during the breeding season. After mating, the female cares for the young alone, while the cock again withdraws into the impassable regions of its living space.

In captivity, after successful acclimation macaws start with courtship toward the end of April, which—in contrast to many other species of birds—is not characterized by special elements of courtship.

The frequency of courtship feeding reaches its peak in the

precopulative phase. An increase in the elements of social grooming can also be observed during this time. The readiness to defend the nest cavity grows; possible intruders, whether people or animals, are violently attacked with raised nape feathers and spread tail and if possible are driven from the territory.

Copulation can be viewed as the final link in the cock's courtship activities. Females display their readiness to mate by crouching down and spreading their wing and tail feathers slightly. As a rule, the hen assumes the position for copulation after prior courtship by the cock; in closely mated birds, parts of courtship behavior may be omitted and copulation may be initiated directly.

The actual mating process can resemble the behavior Dilger (1960) describes for the African parrot genus *Agapornis*: "The cock mounts the hen, fixes its claws in the female's flank feathers, lowers its tail, and through rhythmic movements brings both cloacas together."

Just as often, macaws mate by perching next to each other on a branch, raising their tails, and pressing together the openings of the cloacas, into which the spermatic duct and oviduct open.

Before fertilization occurs, several attempts at mating apparently take place, the frequency of which increases until the eggs are laid.

Courtship lasts about 10 to 14 days. During this time the birds prepare the future nest chamber, which in captivity can consist of a hollowed-out tree trunk.

Eggs are laid in captivity in the

The macaws owned by Linn shown preening (*above*) and in their nest box (*below*).

second half of the month of May. As a rule, the clutch consists of two, more rarely, three or four eggs, which—depending on the species—are incubated by the female for 24 to 28 days.

The freshly hatched young are fed

One of the most evident characteristics of the Scarlet Macaw (*Ara macao*, above and below) is its bare facial skin.

Facing page: Yellow-collared Macaw (*Ara auricollis*).

A trio of Yellow-collared Macaws (*Ara auricollis*) at five weeks of age.

Right: Hyacinth Macaws, (*Anodorhynchus hyacinthinus*).

for the first time by the hen after a few hours. After several days, the cock also takes part in the feeding of the brood.

Depending on the species, the entire development of young macaws lasts three to four months. A further four to six weeks pass before they attain their independence.

Left: These hard-reared young macaws, photographed in the ruins at Palenque, Mexico, are kept by the Indians as house pets.

Purchase

Advice before the Purchase

Before you decide to buy a macaw, various things must be considered carefully. You should never allow yourself to be tempted to buy on impulse because of the beautifully colored appearance or other attribute of such an animal; the consequences of this rarely can be foreseen.

The first thing to consider is whether a suitable space is available for the bird. The large species at best do poorly in the home; they need a suitable indoor or outdoor aviary. Small macaws, on the other hand, are accordingly better suited for keeping in smaller homes. In addition, they give off the acrid, sweetish smell, which clings to the larger species—even when kept scrupulously clean—to a lesser degree.

Another important point is the question of the provision for the bird. Such a macaw needs intensive care by the keeper day after day. It requires fresh water, food, and fruit daily. Furthermore, fresh "gnawing branches" must be obtained at regular intervals, which often proves to be difficult, particularly for the city dweller. The regular cleaning of a large macaw cage also is not always easy for someone who lives in a small apartment. In addition, the care of the bird in the event of illness or during the owner's vacation must be guaranteed.

More or less characteristic of virtually all macaws are the dreadful utterances, which are not always appreciated by impatient neighbors, and often are even perceived as a disturbance of the peace. Before making premature judgments on the neighborly "love of animals," you should keep in mind that large macaw species can deliver real screeching concerts, which can nip in the bud any neighbor's love of animals.

The legal basis that applies here is the federal emissions act (act for the protection against air pollution, noises, an similar environmental

At a length of 85 centimeters, the Blue-throated Macaw (*Ara glaucogularis*) counts as one of the large macaws.

effects) in the version of March 18, 1975:

§ 12 *Keeping of animals*

Animals are to be kept in such a way that no one will be disturbed more than negligibly by the noise produced by them.

It is illegal to act deliberately or negligently contrary to § 12 by not keeping animals in such a way that no one will be disturbed more than negligibly by the noise produced by them.

It is regrettable that parrot fanciers must be confronted with legal strictures in the practice of their fancy. Unfortunately, in a world in which, as a rule, there is no room for animals, such warnings cannot be rejected out of hand.

A singly kept macaw, which is kept as a tame house pet in a cage, needs special attention from its keeper. As soon as the bird has overcome its mistrust towards the new situation after the purchase, it will try to become closely attached to its new keeper. It finally considers him—in the absence of a conspecific—as a mate, which under certain circumstances may seldom be permitted to leave its side. Emotional imbalances, which may be expressed in the form of feather plucking or neurotic screeching, could be the result of a neglected animal–man relationship.

Left: In general, the larger macaws such as the Red-and-green (*Ara chloroptera*) are noisier than the smaller species.

Facing page: Anyone contemplating keeping macaws must reckon with their natural inclination to gnaw. Here, perched on a well-gnawed log, a Blue-and-yellow (*Ara ararauna*) bills with a Red-and-green (*A. chloroptera*).

A final piece of advice should not go unmentioned: a suitable specialist book is recommended to the future macaw keeper, which if possible should be studied before the purchase, in order to achieve a certain level of information. A number of suitable books have been published, which are of assistance in avoiding gross errors in keeping.

Anyone who is still determined to buy a macaw, despite these remarks, must face another hurdle before the purchase: the purchase price of a large macaw of the genus *Ara* (such as a Blue-and-yellow, Red-and-green, Military, or Scarlet Macaw) is notably high, especially for tame and "talking" birds. Small macaw species (Illiger's, Chestnut-fronted, Yellow-collared, and Red-shouldered Macaws) can, however, usually be obtained at a reasonable price, depending on the number of importations at the time.

The Hyacinth Macaw (*Anodorhynchus hyacinthinus*), the only representative of its genus available on the market, is imported only sporadically and then as a rule fetches an extremely high purchase price.

Buying a Bird

You should set about the purchase only when all of this advice has been thought over, when you have already studied a suitable specialist book, and a cage has been bought and furnished.

Although the trade in various animal species has recently become severely limited, at the moment macaws can still be obtained everywhere. As a rule, you will begin the search for a suitable bird in the nearest pet shop; however, they usually do not have a large selection.

Another possibility is the intensive study of relevant specialist journals, where parrots are constantly offered in the advertisement section.

Wholesale dealers (direct importers) are also often willing to sell single birds to private persons. Here the buyer usually finds a large selection of birds from several species. A comparison of prices with those of other dealers is advisable, however, since several importers often offer the same species at different prices.

If an opportunity presents itself to

Singly kept macaws, such as this Blue-and-yellow (*Ara ararauna*), may resort to feather plucking in response to insufficient social stimulus.

buy a captive-bred bird, you should not hesitate long, even if the purchase price is a little higher. Such a bird has been spared from the usual quarantine period and the stress associated with it. In addition, its plumage is in better condition and it will tolerate a Central European climate

difficulties even to experts. There are various criteria, however, which to a large extent reduce the risk of buying a sick bird. Without wishing to question the reliability of the majority of commercial bird dealers, I recommend familiarizing yourself with the following criteria (modified after Ebert, 1978):

Before allowing macaws outdoors, careful acclimation to the local climate is necessary. Here, Hyacinth Macaws (*Anodorhynchus hyacinthinus*) keep to a perch on a Florida patio.

considerably better than will its imported conspecifics. Nevertheless, the number of fanciers who regularly breed macaws is negligible compared to the large number of imported birds. Accordingly, you should always greet the offer of a "captive-bred bird" with a healthy amount of skepticism and insist upon any traits the bird is supposed to display guaranteed in writing.

The actual selection of a healthy bird occasionally presents

Possible Pathological Changes: In Behavior. a) apathy, fluffing of plumage, hiding in a corner on the bottom of the cage or aviary. b) compulsive movements. c) choking, vomiting, defecating with intense pressing and quiet peeping. d) increased nervousness, fussing with plumage, picking at different parts of the body. e) difficulty in breathing with open bill and trembling of the body.

In Carriage. a) curved back, conspicuous flicking or moving of

of an olive-green and a white component). c) failure to defecate.

In addition, a number of other symptoms can indicate illness:

a) not clear, cloudy eyes, combined with one or more of the preceding symptoms. b) assuming the sleeping position conspicuously often, whereby the bird hides its head under a wing, closes the eyes partly or completely, and rests on both legs (again possibly combined with the preceding symptom). c) gummed up nostrils, from which the bird discharges a slimy fluid.

Finally, the bird should be examined for emaciation and claw, toe, and bill deformities. Fairly small toe and claw deformities are no cause for concern and should not keep you from making the purchase. As can be shown, these will not cause problems if the bird is to be bred at a later date.

Birds with bill deformities—even on a fairly small scale—as a rule should not be bought, since unforeseeable problems with food uptake frequently result.

The state of nourishment of a macaw can be determined in two ways: In the first method, the bird is held in the hand and its state of nourishment is determined by exploring the breast with the fingers. If the breast bone protrudes sharply, this is a clear sign of undernourishment. This need not necessarily have threatening effects, however; if a number of birds are present in an aviary, it may be possible that some birds are subordinate to others in the social hierarchy and are therefore usually kept away from the food bowls. If there are no other reasons for this emaciation (such as infestation with

Red-and-green Macaw (*Ara chloroptera*) raising its shoulders—an action that commonly follows a period of inactivity.

the tail up and down, disturbances of equilibrium. b) lameness of legs on one or both sides; weakness in the legs, which is expressed in crouching down on the perch and a slight slipping of the toes; toe curvature up to the extreme case of "forming the feet into a fist." c) lameness of wings on one or both sides, holding wings away from the body.

In Droppings. a) consistency (pasty, watery, hard). b) color (in a healthy bird the droppings consist

Alertness, as is exhibited by this Red-bellied Macaw (*Ara manilata*), is one of the marks of a healthy bird.

A Blue-and-yellow Macaw (*Ara ararauna*). The surface flaking of normal bill growth is more visible in the dark-billed species.

endoparasites or some other illnesses), such a parrot will be in good condition again within a few weeks. The described method of examination can, however, only be used with tame or small macaws.

With the large species, which can be caught and examined only with difficulty, it is advisable to get a general idea of the state of nourishment through weighing. This can be done by weighing the bird together with the transport box upon arrival, and then weighing the empty transport box separately after the bird has been transferred to the cage or aviary. The weights given below have been checked against the average weights for macaws given in Pinter (1979):

Hyacinth Macaws (*Anodorhynchus hyacinthinus*) 900–1400 grams;

Red-and-green Macaws (*Ara chloroptera*) 900–1400 grams;

Scarlet Macaws (*Ara macao*) 800–1000 grams;

Blue-and-yellow Macaws (*Ara ararauna*) 800–1000 grams;

Great Green Macaws (*Ara ambigua*) 800–1000 grams;

Scarlet Macaws (*Ara macao*). Weight loss resulting from illness is first evident on the breast. If possible, a bird's breast should be palpated before purchasing it.

Military Macaws (*Ara militaris*) and comparable species 600–700 grams;

Yellow-collared Macaws (*Ara auricollis*) and comparable species 220–300 grams.

It should be kept in mind that these weights only give an approximate overview. The lower values are to be considered as the

The Hyacinth Macaw (*Anodorhynchus hyacinthinus*) is the largest of the macaw species.

lower limit of the normal range; the higher value as a rule applies to fully grown, several-year-old males.

Special attention should also be given to the condition of the bird's plumage. A parrot that has been obtained on the wholesale or retail market most often exhibits a tattered, worn plumage; often, the flight feathers have been trimmed brutally and the tail feathers have broken off in cramped transport boxes. These features are the order of the day with imported birds—as a result of the capture, shipment, and the time spent in quarantine—and should not deter the buyer from buying such a bird; in most cases, these "blemishes" disappear after the annual molt.

However, with birds that are assuredly several years old and have several complete molts behind them, visible bare spots particularly on the breast, belly, and shoulder region should alert the buyer before purchase—caution should be exercised. Among all large parrots, cockatoos (particularly the large species such as Salmon-crested, White, and large Sulphur-crested cockatoos) and all macaw species are particularly prone to feather plucking, the cause of which has not been conclusively explained to this day. The spectrum of this manifestation extends from occasional plucking of the lesser feathers up to plucking the body completely bare in all accessible places, and even to self-mutilation through gnawing at the skin (see Kronberger, 1978). A combination of the following elements come in question as possible causes:

a) deficient diet. b) suppressed need for movement. c) "boredom,"

Tidy plumage, although a desideratum, should not be a principal concern in selecting a macaw. Minor plumage defects result from transport and are soon repaired. The fine-feathered birds here are Scarlet (*Ara macao*) and Blue-and-yellow (*A. Ararauna*) macaws.

"lack of personal experience." d) unsatisfied breeding drive. e) skin diseases. f) unfavorable climatic conditions in the keeping room. g) psychic disturbances.

In my opinion, point b) is of particular importance. How else can it be explained that particularly the large species of the genus, which from experience are for the most part kept in cages or aviaries that are too small, are far more likely to acquire this "vice"?

It is recommended to adjust keeping conditions to the needs of the bird from the start, in order to prevent a problem of this kind.

Once the parrot has started with feather plucking, it is difficult—if not impossible—to break it of the habit.

Diagram of a Transport Box

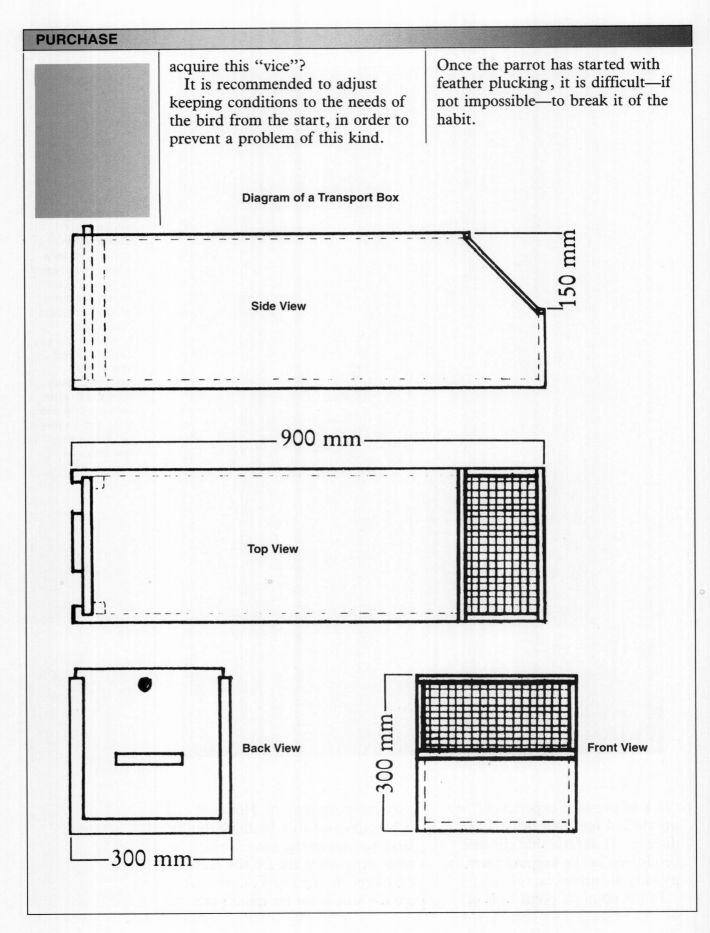

Side View

900 mm

Top View

Back View

300 mm

150 mm

300 mm

Front View

Accommo-dations

If after careful consideration you have finally decided to obtain a bird, it is best to bring it to its future home promptly in a transport box of the appropriate size. Such a container, if possible, should be enclosed on all sides except for a slanted air hatch covered with wire mesh, and should be constructed of a sturdy material, which will be able to stand up to the strong bills of the macaws for a certain amount of time.

Transport in a usual parrot cage is not recommended, so as not to upset the bird through constantly changing impressions—for example, on a fairly long trip by car—and to prevent frightened fluttering.

Upon arrival the bird will first be kept in a prepared cage or a small indoor aviary, preferably separated from any other animals that could be present.

Here the new arrival will be observed closely for several weeks. During this time it is advisable to collect specimens of the bird's droppings twice at intervals of three weeks. These will then be sent—as fresh and unsoiled as possible—in a sealed, air-tight glass vial to a veterinary institute for bacteriological and parasitological examination. If these tests yield a positive result, the bird must receive appropriate treatment before it is added to the remaining stock. When treatment has been completed, another examination of the droppings is necessary. During the time the new acquisition is kept in isolation, the keeper

Red-shouldered Macaw (*Ara nobilis*). Newly arrived birds should be quartered so that close observation is possible for a time.

simultaneously has the opportunity to become familiar with the peculiarities of the bird.

There are usually no difficulties in the feeding of a bird purchased from a wholesale supplier, especially since all legally imported parrots have completed a prescribed quarantine period of 45 days, in which they have been slowly accustomed to the parrot food usual in the trade. Possible deviations (e.g., the exclusive feeding of one kind of seed) should be corrected "intuitively."

It should also be pointed out that, after newly imported parrots are transferred to an official quarantine station, they are kept at a fairly high room temperature, and are only slowly acclimated to normal room temperatures in the course of the prescribed quarantine period. Such birds still need heated accommodations after they have passed through quarantine and cannot be moved to an outdoor aviary immediately. At first they should be placed outside only by the hour in warm weather.

Once the newly acquired parrot has been moved in with other birds after the period of observation, it will at first be quite susceptible to the problems of its new environment, which can be caused by the other inhabitants of the aviary, the unfamiliar accommodations, the hierarchy at the food bowls, and so forth. For this reason, it should be given special attention in the daily inspection of the stock, and any difficulties that arise should be remedied.

After the acclimation period, large parrots as a rule are robust, hardy birds, which are not harmed even by fairly cool temperatures. This process of acclimation is finally over, however, only when the birds start molting yearly in the fall, which can often take many years. At this time the feathers that have become very tattered during the breeding season are shed and replaced, so that a complete plumage is again present before winter, which ensures that the bird will be well insulated against the cold.

Accommodations

Various accommodations are suitable for keeping macaws. Most small macaws should be kept in roomy cages. The majority of the models available on the market are,

Fluffed feathers, seen here on a Yellow-collared Macaw (*Ara auricollis*), may be seen during acclimation. Possibly a sign of stress, it bears watching.

In bird parks, the large macaws, which are sedentary in their habits, are often kept unenclosed.

however, unsuitable for this purpose because of their small size. A recommendable cage must exhibit a size of 1.5 × 1.0 × 1.5 meters (length by width by height) in order to hold a bird of this kind. The practicality of the cage should be given consideration when making the purchase. In addition, aspects of hygiene should also be considered.

The furnishings should consist of several hardwood perches of different diameters as well as three or four securely attached food bowls, which as far as possible should be installed in the upper part of the cage. Glazed ceramic flowerpot saucers, which can be obtained in many sizes and are easy to clean, have proved particularly effective for this purpose.

Also practical are bottom trays, which ensure the thorough cleaning of the floor of the cage. Builder's

The size and gauge of wire mesh employed in a flight for macaws should suit the species housed. These are Chestnut-fronted Macaws (*Ara severa*).

over outdoor flights. First, the neighbors are for the most part spared the often terrible screeching produced by these large birds. Particularly in early morning—one of the times of peak activity of the parrots—the windows can be kept closed to at least prevent too much noise. A second advantage is the usually straightforward heating of a bird room, which in most cases will be installed inside a centrally heated house.

Basically any room or a space in the cellar is suitable, as long as there is sufficient light and air. In regard to size, an area of 2×4 meters should be considered as the minimum for a pair of the larger species.

Wallpaper or other coverings should be removed from the walls and ceiling, which should then be painted with a non-toxic white paint. The windows are covered with bars on the inside, to prevent the birds from escaping should the glass happen to break. Furthermore, in this way the birds are prevented from flying against the panes, which they do not recognize as glass, and injuring themselves.

The furnishing of a bird room can be quite spartan. Besides several food bowls and a large, stable bathing dish, a few branches of different diameters with side shoots, which satisfy the parrots' need to gnaw, are sufficient. The actual perches should consist of hardwood and should be installed as widely spaced as possible, in order to force the birds to make short flights. Perches of steel pipe, which are used time and again by private fanciers as well as in zoos because of

sand, which is available at any home center, is suitable as a substrate, as is the special bird sand, available at pet shops, which is sterilized at high temperatures and has the addition of anise to reduce the odor produced by the birds. Cages have less to recommend them for use with larger macaws, which need several meters of flight space and consequently can only be kept in roomy bird rooms or outdoor flights.

Bird rooms have two advantages

A Red-and-green Macaw (*Ara chloroptera*) enjoys a banana. Food is best offered in heavy dishes that can be securely fixed to a perch or the wire.

their durability, are completely unsuitable.

Roomy outdoor aviaries provide an ideal environment for all macaw species—as long as certain rules are followed. A basic requirement for successful keeping is, however, the presence of a heatable security house. No wood at all may be used in the construction of macaw enclosures, since all species are heavy gnawers. A shelter room built of brick on a winterproof, steel-reinforced concrete slab would be considered ideal. To lower the cost of heating, it is strongly advised to insulate the roof and exterior walls. In addition to well-tried fiberglass, Styropor®, which is available in various thicknesses, has become the most widely used form of insulation. Plastic-coated sheet metal or sheet asbestos can be used as an exterior covering. The size of the interior space should not be less than 2 × 2 meters.

The outdoor aviary must be provided with light, running water, and a heat source. The heating of such an aviary can be accomplished in various ways. The simplest and least expensive method is to connect the aviary to the central heating of the house; the importance of good insulation cannot be over stressed. If not connected to the central heating of the home, electric heaters can do good service.

For the construction of the outdoor flight, which is attached to the security house and is connected with it by means of a 30 × 30-centimeter hatch, galvanized pipe as well as so-called square pipe with a width of 40 to 50 millimeters are suitable, which as a rule are welded together on the spot into a framework for the aviary. Another

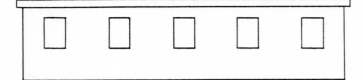

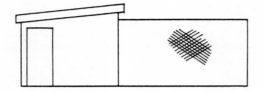

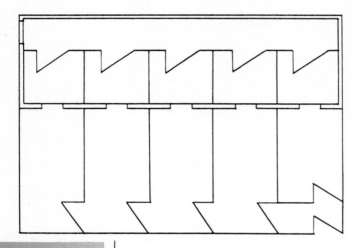

Diagram of an aviary. *Top*: Exterior elevation showing windows into the service corridor, one window for each shelter. *Middle*: Side elevation depicting shelter section with door and wire-walled flight portion. *Bottom*: Floor plan showing service corridor, and five shelter-and-flight sections.

keep vermin out of the enclosure.

Building a double covering of wire mesh is a way—albeit a costly one—to solve this problem. For the inside covering of an aviary for small macaws, rectangular galvanized wire mesh with 25 millimeters between strands and a wire thickness of 1.75 millimeters is used. For large macaw species, so-called "wavy" wire mesh (in various styles and dimensions) and galvanized rigid wire mesh (50 millimeters between strands, 4 millimeters thick) are suitable. The outside covering consists of rectangular wire mesh with 12.7 millimeters between strands (wire thickness 1.05 millimeters). This keeps all kinds of vermin, even half-grown mice, out of the aviary.

One-third of the roof of the flight is covered with transparent plastic to offer the birds protection against rain. The floor of the outdoor aviary must be equipped either with cement flagstones laid without joints or with a solid concrete foundation, which is easy to clean.

The frequently recommended practice of keeping birds on a natural floor in my opinion leads to some problems. Besides making it easier for vermin—chiefly rats—to enter the aviary, there are also virtually unsolvable problems with the cleaning and disinfection of the enclosure. The need to dig up the natural floor to a depth of 20 to 30 centimeters and to replace the soil yearly will certainly not excite any bird keeper; there is also no lasting guarantee that the parasites in the soil will be exterminated. For this purpose, Gewalt (1969) recommends using a blow torch to kill pathogens in the soil.

possibility is the frame design recommended by Delphy (1975). He suggests building aviaries out of individual frames with a size of 2 × 1 meters (height by width), which can be replaced at any time. Using this method it is even possible to dismantle the entire structure or change the ground plan at little expense. The cost of materials—because of the fairly large requirement for iron pipe—is, however, considerably higher.

There is a small problem in the selection of the wire mesh, since at the moment there is no type of mesh on the market which can withstand the strong bills of macaws as well as

The aviary complex is furnished in the same way as the bird room. The food table and possible nesting facilities are to be installed in the shelter room. At an average width of two meters, the length of the aviary should vary—depending on the species of macaw—between two and six meters. If several aviaries are erected side by side, it is practical to separate the individual compartments from one another by means of opaque partitions. It is also recommended to install an aisle in the shelter room to permit access to the individual compartments.

Macaws, particularly the large species of the genus *Ara*, as well as the Hyacinth Macaw, with their flight feathers trimmed on one side, are often kept on large climbing trees, which as a rule they hardly ever leave. Using this method, which is now practiced by some fanciers and zoos, macaws often become gradually acclimated to liberty, which in my opinion—with certain qualifications—offers ideal keeping conditions. However, experiments of this kind can only be carried out successfully in rural areas, where the various consequences of "civilization" cannot cause the birds any injury.

Dubbert (personal correspondence), the former director of the Metelen bird park, learned the following from the experiments with such an arrangement: The birds first searched for a partner within the fairly large flock of macaws. Only after successful pairing was one of the two birds put at liberty, while the mate's wings were trimmed so that it could not leave the climbing tree. The reverse was done the following year, so that the bird kept at liberty until then lost most of its flying ability, while the other bird, the flight feathers of which had grown back, was kept at liberty. Only in the third year were both birds kept together at liberty in the park. Even though a bird occasionally wandered off, the majority of the parrots stayed in the immediate vicinity of the large macaw meadow, which was furnished with climbing trees.

The large species of the genus *Ara*—especially the Blue-and-yellow Macaw—are described by Bedford (1954) as extremely sedentary and thus particularly suited for liberty.

A tame Blue-and-yellow Macaw (*Ara ararauna*) about to step onto an offered perch.

81

The acclimation of Hyacinth Macaws to liberty proves to be more difficult and cannot be recommended.

The keeping of macaws on so-called hanging perches, in which the birds are prevented from escaping either by means of a chain or through the amputation of part of a wing, is often observed. Gewalt (1969) mentions the example of a large curlew, which had its ability to fly taken from it in this way. This form of keeping must be considered as inappropriate, and on principle it should not be advocated.

Gnawing the bark off a natural perch may provide a macaw with useful nutrients, in addition to keeping it occupied. This is the Red-and-green Macaw (*Ara chloroptera*).

Finally, a problem mentioned by Arndt (1981) merits discussion. It is based on the fact that the extremely intelligent parrots are offered too little sensory stimulation as a result of the sterile environment of conventional aviaries. Furnishing the aviary with branched climbing

them in pairs during the breeding season. It is advisable to provide a separate aviary for each pair to prevent other aviary occupants from disrupting breeding attempts.

Community keeping is only conditionally possible and basically can only be used for displaying the

For a successful bird show, a close rapport between the macaw and the handler must have been established. Here, a Red-and-green Macaw (*Ara chloroptera*).

branches, swings, chains, ropes, and so forth, can keep the birds occupied at all times and prevents the dreaded plucking and other psychological disturbances.

If macaws are kept for breeding purposes, it is essential to keep

birds. An aviary in which several macaws are to be kept must be much larger than normal to allow the birds to occupy and defend an individual space and to provide room for subordinate individuals to escape from attack.

Risa Teitler has been a parrot trainer at Parrot Jungle in Miami, Florida. Besides other large macaw species, Hyacinth Macaws (*Anodorhynchus hyacinthinus*) have been found to be especially teachable.

When offered a hand, this tame Blue-and-yellow Macaw (*Ara ararauna*) will step up onto it.

A truly tame macaw, such as this Blue-and-yellow (*Ara ararauna*), will allow itself to be touched freely. Similarly, it understands that it must be gentle in applying its beak to human flesh.

For feeding this Blue-and-yellow Macaw (*Ara ararauna*), a metal food dish has been welded to the perch.

Diet

Besides appropriate accommodations, a balanced, varied diet is of special significance for maintaining the health of animals kept in captivity. If you consider what an extensive supply of food is available to macaws living in their tropical homeland, the selection of foods offered in captivity can at best have a substitute character. Nevertheless, the knowledgeable bird keeper has numerous possibilities for developing a varied menu for his feathered charges. The longevity of many large parrots in captivity, which often live a human life span, proves that dietary and physiological problems in keeping parrots are certainly solvable.

Just as do other animals, parrots also require as basic nutrients: fats, carbohydrates, and proteins. In addition, they need vitamins, minerals, trace elements, and fiber. All of these components are present in sufficient amounts in a properly planned diet, even though the proportion of the individual basic nutrients in the total amount of food consumed can vary greatly from bird to bird. In exceptional cases, a bird may eat large amounts of a particular food daily, but because of the minimal nutritional value could nevertheless become emaciated and in extreme cases starve. Since the sense of taste is well developed in parrots, a bird initially will eat whatever tastes best to it. Nutritious food often will not even be touched if it does not taste as good.

Basic Food

Precise data on the diet of wild macaws unfortunately are not yet available. It is known, though, that they are not marked dietary specialists. They are principally vegetarian and feed on fruits, berries, nuts, buds, and other nutriments. They are most often observed eating fruits of palms and figs. In addition, the remains of insects of various kinds have been found in the crops of dissected birds.

A large portion of the food offered in captivity consists of seeds. The composition of a suitable

mixture is dependent on the nutritive content of the individual components. Not counting exceptions, the seeds that come into consideration can be divided into starchy and oily types.

Starchy types include oats, wheat, maize, and rice. Their fat content varies between two and five percent, the carbohydrate content is between 55 and 60 percent, and the raw protein content is 10 to 12 percent. To the oily seeds belong sunflower seeds, nuts, hemp, and beech nuts (fat content, 20 to 50 percent; carbohydrate content, six to 21 percent; protein content ten to 20 percent).

Among these foods, sunflower seeds are of the greatest significance for the feeding of parrots. Because of the small percentage of raw fiber they contain, they are easily digested by the birds. Also beneficial is the content of raw fat, raw protein, and minerals.

Reproduced below is the seed

Nut shells of the kind shown here are opened by Hyacinth Macaws (*Anodorhynchus hyacinthinus*) in order to consume the kernel.

A macaw, such as this Red-and-green (*Ara chloroptera*), is able to use its foot to bring food to the bill.

mixture for large parrots recommended by Pinter (1979), which has proved effective in practice:

sunflower seeds 70%

oats, raw rice, maize, peanuts, pumpkin seeds, total of 30%

In addition, this mixture can be varied by adding wheat, hemp, beech nuts, hazel nuts, and cembra-pine nuts, whereby the percentage of sunflower seeds should remain the same. Small seeds like canary seed and millet are also suitable for small macaws.

When purchasing food, special attention must be paid to the condition of the seeds. You should select ripe, well-dried seeds, the surfaces of which are smooth and dust-free.

All oily nuts and seeds have only a limited shelf life, even if stored properly, and become rancid sooner or later. Spoiled seeds can be dangerous for the birds and can cause severe indigestion. For this reason they should only be stored in limited quantities.

Sprouted Food, Fruit, and Greenfood

It is known that parrots in the wild not only feed on dry, ripe seeds, but also on seeds in various stages of ripeness or even in sprouted form. This information should be given consideration in captivity, especially since half-ripe seeds are particularly nutritious because of their vitamin, mineral, and protein content.

First and foremost there is maize, which—particularly in a half-ripe state—is greatly appreciated by most parrots. Unfortunately, fresh ears of maize are available only in late summer; anyone who has a freezer, however, can freeze appropriate amounts for the winter. It is most practical to begin with the feeding of small amounts, since the sudden addition of a supplement of this kind can lead to indigestion. In addition, there are cultivated plants like oats, wheat, millet, as well as wild plants, the seeds of which can be used in a half-ripe state.

Another important food, which can be very valuable particularly in winter or during breeding season, is sprouted seeds. Oats, wheat, and sunflower seeds are the most suitable for sprouting. The required amount is put in a container with water and left there for 24 hours to pre-germinate. After that the seeds are rinsed thoroughly under running water and are spread out on mesh-covered frames. After a further 24 to 36 hours—depending on temperature—the sprouts will have broken through and can be fed

Today, parrot foods are carefully formulated to provide a balanced and nutritionally complete diet. Photo courtesy of Rolf C. Hagen.

This Blue-and-yellow Macaw (*Ara ararauna*) has been trained to pull up the bowl to obtain the food reward inside.

after a final rinsing.

The feeding of fruit and greenfood is also important for a varied diet. Apples, pears, carrots, cherries, strawberries, red currants, raspberries, and plums are just as suitable as exotic fruits like bananas, oranges, pineapple, kiwi fruit, and so forth. A rich palette of suitable plants is available as greenfood. Parsley has a very high

vitamin and mineral content. In addition, endive, spinach, lettuce, stock beet, lamb's lettuce, and much more besides are available. Certain wild weeds like dandelion (*Taraxacum vulgare*), shepherd's purse (*Capsella burs-pastoris*), plantain (*Plantago*), and especially chickweed (*Stellaria media*) are recommended.

Animal Food

In addition to vegetable food products, in the wild parrots also feed on small amounts of animal food. This can be taken into account in the composition of the diet. Recommended are ant eggs and dried shrimp, which are also used for feeding chickens. The latter are always available on the market at a reasonable price and can be mixed with the previously mentioned seeds.

In addition, mealworms, which are well liked by some large parrots, are also suitable; however, they should not be offered in large

The staple seed diet for macaws can be easily be enhanced with products that contain additionally nutritionally significant ingredients. Photo courtesy of Rolf C. Hagen.

quantities.

Hard-boiled egg, raw or cooked meat, among other things, are also prized as sources of protein by many psittacids and can occasionally be offered in small amounts.

exhibit a moist-crumbly consistency as a result of the addition of fat supplements.

Kronberger (1978) advises the feeding of low-fat dry cottage cheese, mixed with a commercial egg food. You can make your own

The peanut is another favorite food of macaws. These are some of the variously colored interspecific hybrids bred at Parrot Jungle in Miami, Florida.

Supplemental Food

Particularly during the breeding season, it is advisable to offer the parrots a supplemental mixture of soft food. Various mixtures are available on the market, which are obtainable under the names rearing food, egg food, or soft bill food. Soft bill food is a protein-rich dry food to which dried insects, ant pupae, vitamins and minerals have been added, and which is fed in a dry or moistened state. Also on the market are types of soft food that

suitable soft food by pulverizing a hard-boiled egg and mixing it with zwieback, edible calcium, and vitamins.

The amount offered must never be greater than can be eaten within a few hours, since spoiled food can have a toxic effect and is particularly dangerous for youngsters.

It is advisable to offer the food in shallow and, if possible, round containers, which can be cleaned easily.

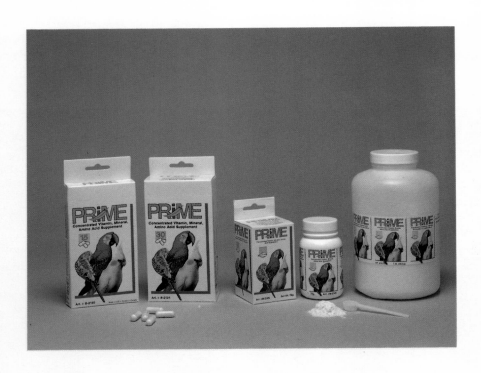

Minerals and Vitamins

The need for minerals can be satisfied through the supplemental feeding of edible calcium. This contains trace elements like phosphorus, magnesium, iodine, iron, copper, manganese, and cobalt, among others. It should be offered year 'round in a separate bowl. In addition, boiled, crushed egg shells or cuttlebone, which is obtained from squid, are also suitable.

The sand used to cover the floor of the cage as well as grit allow the birds to take up small stones, which they require for pulverizing food in the ventriculus.

With the regular feeding of the basic and supplemental foods, symptoms of vitamin deficiency will scarcely ever occur. Nevertheless, it is advisable—above all during the yearly molt—to offer supplemental multi-vitamin preparations. Numerous preparations are available on the market and can be given to the birds in the soft food or drinking water. Caution is advised in the administering of Vitamin D, since an overdose can have most detrimental effects, or at worse, fatal consequences.

Since many vitamins lose their effect after fairly long storage, attention must always be given to the expiration date.

Symptoms of vitamin deficiency

Nutritional Analysis of Greenfoods

Nutrients in a 100-gram edible portion	Main Components			Minerals					Vitamins			
	Protein	Fat	Carbo-hydrate	Sodium	Potassium	Calcium	Phos-phorus	Iron	A	B_1	B_2	C
	g	g	g	mg	mg	mg	mg	mg	IU	mcg	mcg	mg
Head Lettuce	1.2	0.2	1.7	8	220	20	35	0.6	1500	60	90	10
Endive	1.7	0.2	2.0	50	350	50	50	1.4	900	52	120	9
Spinach	2.4	0.4	2.4	60	660	110	48	3.0	8200	86	240	47
Mangel	2.1	0.3	2.9	90	380	100	40	2.7	5900	100	160	40
Lamb's Quarters	1.8	0.4	2.6	4	420	30	50	2.0	7000	65	80	30
Parsley	4.4	0.4	9.8	30	1000	240	130	8.0	12080	140	300	170
Carrots	1.0	0.2	7.3	45	280	35	30	0.7	13500	70	55	6
Red Beets	1.5	0.1	7.6	86	340	30	45	0.9	180	22	40	10
Radish	1.0	0.1	3.5	17	255	34	26	1.5	38	33	30	30

(so-called avitamintosis) are common illnesses in cage birds, which—if untreated—not infrequently lead to death. The symptoms of these illnesses are presented in the following section. The tabulation is taken from the work by Pinter (1979).

Vitamin A deficiency Affected mucous membranes, watering eyes, whitish deposits of the cornea, infertility, poor growth of youngsters.

Vitamin B deficiency Disorders of the central nervous system (for example, inability to fly, uncoordinated body movements, and convulsions).

Vitamin C deficiency Abnormal sensitivity of the mucous membranes, reduced resistance to illness.

Right: Feeding station for the macaws at Parrot Jungle.

Below: This Red-and-green Macaw (*Ara chloroptera*) has been taught how to plant a flower.

Vitamin D deficiency Disorders in the development of the skeleton in young birds (rachitis).

Vitamin E deficiency Infertility; severe deficiency can lead to muscular atrophy in young birds.

Vitamin K deficiency Reduction in the clotting ability of the blood.

Vitamin G deficiency Disorders in the development of the plumage.

Care

Cleaning the Cage and Aviary

Regular cleaning of the accommodations is essential for the successful keeping of animals in captivity. The cage of a singly kept house pet must be cleaned thoroughly at least once a week. Whereas the top part of the cage can be sprayed off in the shower or with a hose in the garden, the tray for collecting droppings is emptied, scrubbed out thoroughly with hot water, and finally disinfected. Only after drying should a new layer of sand be spread on the bottom. Tree branches of appropriate thickness serve as perches, which are replaced with fresh ones weekly. The food and water bowls must also be cleaned thoroughly with hot water.

After all the parts of the cage are completely dry, the bird, which was kept somewhere else (for example, on its climbing tree) during cleaning, can return to its housing.

Depending on how soiled they become, aviaries are raked out once or twice a week with a leaf rake and furnished with a new layer of sand, if necessary. From time to time, tiled indoor flights can be sprayed out with a garden hose and disinfected. If the floor of the outdoor flight is not made of cement flagstones, the soil must be dug over once a year or replaced occasionally.

Care of the Plumage

In addition to the regular cleaning of accommodations, the bird must also be sprayed once or several times a week. With cage birds this is done by spraying them with a plant sprayer. Newly acquired parrots shrink back from this procedure at first and with loud screeching seek refuge in a corner of the cage. Once the bird has gotten accustomed to the process, however, it will appreciate the shower and will express its well-being by spreading its wings and tail

Wire mesh, employed in the housing of this Red-fronted Macaw (*Ara rubrogenys*), can be cleaned by scrubbing it with a brush.

feathers. It can now be placed in the bathtub or shower together with the top part of the cage or on a perch and sprayed with lukewarm water.

It is best to perform the shower in the morning, so that the bird is dry again by evening. During this time you should make sure that the temperature of the room is high enough. Aviary birds will—if given

the opportunity—sometimes perch in a warm summer rain; in addition, they can also be sprayed from time to time with a garden hose. For larger aviary installations, it is advisable to install a sprinkler.

Trimming Claws and Bill Tip

Before the correct procedures for the trimming of the claws and bill are described, there follows a brief description of how to catch and secure a macaw for this and other health-keeping procedures.

Heavy leather gloves are necessary for catching aviary birds as well as finger-tame cage birds which do not allow themselves to be held without struggling violently. The parrot is grasped on the nape quickly from behind, with the thumb and index finger holding the head still, while the rest of the hand firmly surrounds the wings to prevent fluttering. Now you allow the bird to bite on a wooden dowel with its bill and also make sure that

the legs are supported. Only now can the planned procedure be started, and it is best carried out with a helper—particularly with the larger species, one person literally has his hands full trying to secure the struggling bird.

In captivity it occasionally happens—particularly with birds kept as house pets—that the claws are not worn away enough and thus hamper the bird in its efforts to clasp onto its perch. Furthermore, such birds face the increased danger that the overly long claws will get caught in the wire mesh and they will injure themselves.

By furnishing the cage appropriately (for example, by using rough tree branches as perches), the bird keeper can support the natural wearing of the claws. Elongated claws are trimmed with normal nail clippers, whereby the location of the cut must not be in the area of the blood vessel, which runs through each claw. While it is possible to see the blood-filled vessels in various small parrots by holding the claws up to a source of light, as a rule this is not possible with macaws, which generally have dark-colored claws, and the keeper must proceed with intuition and a practiced eye. Should bleeding occur despite all precautions, it must be staunched with a suitable medication or a swab that promotes blood clotting (a swab soaked in a ferric-chloride solution).

It is rarely necessary to trim an overly long upper mandible, as long as the bird is given ample opportunity to wear its bill by supplying provisions for gnawing. If a correction proves necessary, it can also be carried out with nail clippers; here again attention must be paid to the location of the blood vessels. The points and edges that are left after the removal of the surplus horn must be smoothed with a nail file. The lower mandible generally does not grow too long, since the bird can whet it on the rasplike grooves of the upper mandible.

Bill deformities, on the other hand, are usually the result of problems with metabolism; possible causes include vitamin, mineral, and protein deficiencies. For this reason, in addition to correcting the horn of the bill, the diet should always be evaluated.

A parrot keeper who does not think he can perform the techniques described above should call in an experienced bird keeper or a veterinarian.

As one person restrains the Blue-and-yellow Macaw (*Ara ararauna*), carefully holding its beak closed, another smooths its claws with a nail file.

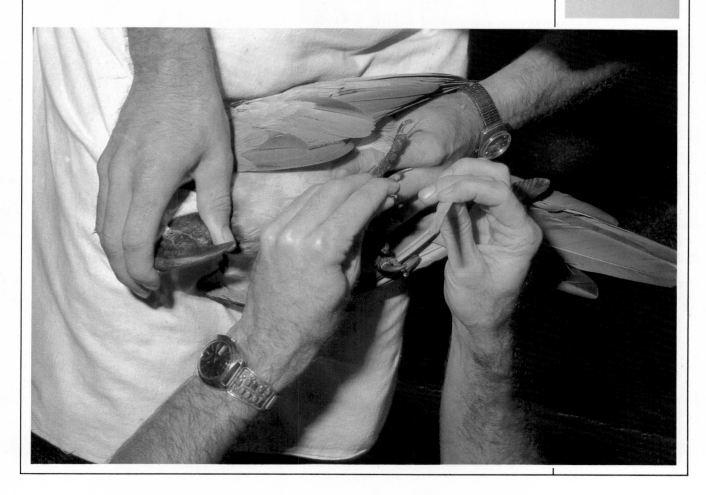

Trimming the Wings

If a macaw is to be kept at liberty in the house or on a climbing tree in the garden, limiting its full flying ability by trimming its flight feathers is required. Nevertheless, you should be absolutely certain beforehand that this procedure is necessary, since it often takes over a year for all of the feathers to grow back again.

A macaw's flight feathers can be trimmed with scissors.

or twice a year.

Trimming only one wing is not advisable, since the macaw somersaults and falls to the ground like a stone when it tries to fly. If, in contrast, both wings are trimmed, it is still capable of gliding short distances, and under certain circumstances—although with difficulty—it can reach safety from unforeseen dangers.

It is advisable to trim the secondaries as well as the inner primaries on both wings. In this way the flying ability of the bird is greatly limited, but nothing can be seen of the trimmed feathers when they are held to the body. The feather sheaths of the trimmed feathers fall out after a while and are replaced with new, functional feathers, so that a trimming correction must be performed once

In my opinion, the severing of the flight muscle tendon or the amputation of part of a wing cannot be considered a measure worthy of consideration by the responsible, humane bird keeper.

Removal of Bands

After leaving a legal quarantine station, every macaw wears a sturdy metal band onto which dates have been stamped, which at any time can provide information on the provenance of the bird.

In some cases such a band, because of improper application or the wrong size, can fit too tightly on the foot and cause inflammation and swelling. In the worst case, the blood flow is obstructed above the band and the part of the foot below dies and/or must be amputated by a veterinarian. Thus, when a macaw is purchased, it is advisable to determine the band size and condition and whether removal of of the band is necessary. It must, however, be saved as documentation.

To remove the band, the bird is held in the correct manner and the banded foot is immobilized with the assistance of a second person. Now the band is turned with the open side toward the observer and the split ends of the band are spread apart a few millimeters using pincers. The gap that is produced in this way is wide enough to insert a snap-ring or C-ring pliers, which will spread the band apart effortlessly. I have tested the described method many times and it rules out any possibility of injuring the bird. The use of two pliers, with which a band of this kind can also be removed by force, can cause skin abrasions or even injuries to the leg bone.

The method proposed by Bosch and Wedde (1981), in which two clamps that can be screwed together are attached like pincers to the ends of the band and are screwed together, thereby making it easier to pull apart the ends of the band, I consider to be extremely complicated as well as dangerous to the bird.

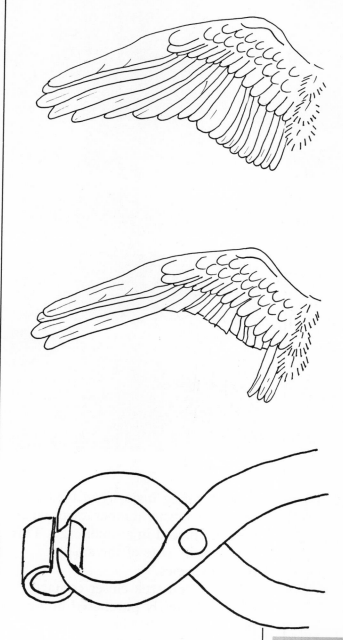

Above: **Feather trimming: To restrict flying ability, trim the inner primaries and some of the secondary feathers.** *Bottom:* **Pincers placed at the seam are used to spread a leg band for removal.**

Taming and Mimicking

If a newly purchased macaw is not earmarked for future breeding attempts, but rather is to be kept as a house pet, sooner or later it will only give its owner pleasure when it has overcome its shyness. Although a few birds reach the importers in a tame or half-tame condition, the

This Blue-and-yellow Macaw (*Ara ararauna*), like other parrots, uses its bill to test fingers and other objects.

overwhelming majority of birds display a stormy temperament when they are placed in a small cage. This is especially true of the smaller macaw species.

Before you seek closer contact with your newly purchased house pet, it should first be left completely undisturbed for a few days. Sudden movements, loud noises, or similar unfamiliar actions are to be avoided in its immediate vicinity. At feeding time, the keeper should talk to the bird in a reassuring tone of voice.

After a short time the macaw begins to feel safe in its new accommodations and no longer flutters around in fright in the cage

as soon as a member of the household approaches. Now the time has come to accustom the bird to the keeper's hand: slowly time and time again a particularly well-liked food item (a peanut, a grape, etc.) is offered by hand through the bars. Here the owner's patience is often given a stern test. Sooner or later the macaw will not be able to resist the temptation and will take the offered treat from the hand.

Attempts of this kind should never be carried out with gloves from fear of biting, since many parrots have had bad experiences with gloves during their capture and transport and hide in a corner of the cage while screeching loudly. If the bird no longer retreats, you should try with great care to have it climb onto your hand. You open the cage door and without haste stretch out the extended arm to it. If it does not climb onto your hand on its own, you should move the hand slowly towards it and force it in this way either to fly away or climb onto your hand. If the bird's flight feathers are trimmed, after several attempts to escape, which as a rule end by falling to the bottom of the cage, it will prefer climbing onto your hand to toppling to the cage floor. Only when the bird no longer shrinks back from the hand can you attempt to take it out of the cage.

The next step is the touching and later the scratching of the bird. At first it will not like being touched at all, and will express its annoyance by striking with its bill. How soon the bird will stop resisting and become completely attached to its owner depends on the bird's age and condition as well as the keeper's patience. Often the bird's attachment will go so far that it considers the keeper as its "mate" and demands of him different proofs of his affection from the sphere of social behavior (for example, the scratching of various parts of the body substitutes for social grooming). If the keeper does not meet these demands, the bird pines away and shows its displeasure through screeching, feather plucking, or some other vice.

Such psychologically damaged parrots, which often change owners several times in succession, are the sad result of poorly executed taming efforts, and should serve to temper the wish to own a "super tame"

bird.

The mimicking ability of different macaw species is considerable, although the clearness of what is repeated falls short of the "performance" of Grey Parrots (*Psittacus erithacus*) of average ability. The mimicking abilities of the Blue-and-yellow Macaw, Scarlet Macaw, Red-and-green Macaw, and Chestnut-fronted Macaw, in particular, are documented in literature.

As a rule, only those birds that are young when they reach people's hands will develop into good "talkers." The best suited are of course birds that were bred in captivity, so that their true age is

A macaw's natural interest in brightly colored objects can be channeled into amusing tricks. Here a Blue-and-yellow Macaw is using a telephone.

Repetition is the basis of speech training: here the owner repeats words to a Red-and-green Macaw (*Ara chloroptera*).

known. Sex plays only a subordinate role in large parrots, whereas in parakeets and small parrots, males are clearly more talented.

The technique of training a bird to talk is relatively simple. The desired words are repeated as clearly as possible to the bird several times a day; at first mainly words with several vowels should be selected.

Sooner or later, as if from out of the blue, the bird will reproduce these words. Depending on the bird's ability, in the course of several months it will then learn the series of sounds and words which it has picked up some place or other, and will later repeat them at every appropriate (and inappropriate) opportunity. The repertoire ranges from the mimicking of the most diverse noises up to the reproduction of human words and sentences.

At the same time, however, you should not forget that a parrot never understands the meaning of its "words," even though it sometimes seems that way. Nevertheless, parrots differ from other mimics in that they can associate a particular activity or sound with a particular word and thus repeat it in a seemingly appropriate place (see Wennrich, 1983). The evening hours are recommended as the time of day for speech training; apparently a parrot's ability to concentrate is greatest then.

A tame macaw is content to remain perched on its owner's hand. *Above*, a Scarlet Macaw (*Ara macao*); *below*, a Red-and-green Macaw (*A. chloroptera*).

Above: Once acclimated to local conditions, macaws are not prone to illness and are usually long-lived. A Scarlet Macaw (*Ara macao*).

Below: With birds as with people, recovery from minor illnesses can be facilitated with over-the-counter medicines, available at a pet shop. Photo courtesy of Rolf C. Hagen.

Illnesses

After careful acclimation, large parrots as a rule are not very susceptible to illness. Good keeping conditions, together with a certain degree of cleanliness, provide for an exceptional resistance to illness and hold losses to a minimum. For all that, birds of course occasionally become ill even in well-managed stocks. The symptoms are usually quite unspecific and can indicate illnesses of different kinds. Fluffed plumage, apathy, emaciation, reduced food intake, change in the consistency of droppings, and others are symptoms that indicate a serious general illness and make it necessary to consult a veterinarian.

Small-animal veterinarians often are completely unqualified to treat birds, so in most cases it is advisable to visit one of the few veterinary specialists for bird diseases found currently in the nation. Although this can be relatively expensive— alone because of the long trip—the cost is worth it with valuable birds.

Bird fanciers are inclined to treat their sick birds themselves at first, and call in a specialist only when they are unsuccessful. Such self-attempts must, however, be strongly advised against, since incorrectly treated and, thus under certain circumstances, chronically ill birds as a rule can no longer be cured even by an expert, whereas if the proper therapy is started in time, many illnesses can be positively influenced.

In the same way, the practice of regularly mixing small doses of an antibiotic in the parrot's food must be warned against. The intended effect, an increase in the bird's powers of resistance, soon produces the opposite effect and leads to a decrease in resistance.

Nevertheless, the knowledgeable animal keeper should initiate various measures when an illness is noticed: first of all, the bird should be isolated from other birds to prevent the transmission of the illness to other conspecifics. In addition, heat irradiation is recommended, through the use of an infrared lamp, which, together with vitamin supplements, soon clears up colds and other minor illnesses.

When encountering symptoms of serious illness, a veterinarian must be visited without delay. Before treatment is started, as long as the bird's condition does not preclude it, a sample of its droppings should be taken and sent to an institute of animal medicine for bacteriological and parasitological examination.

If a bird dies, it should be given to an expert for dissection in the interest of maintaining the health of the remaining stock. Even though there are costs associated with an examination of this kind, the cause of death is most usually determined, and this knowledge can help to avoid further mishaps or errors in keeping in the future.

In past years a number of specialists in animal medicine have studied avian medicine in depth and have published their experiences. In particular, reference should be made to the works of Ebert (1972), Heidenreich (1980), Kemna (1976), Dronberger (1971), and Raethel (1968).

Macaw fanciers are urged to pair their birds, with a view toward captive propagation. Red-and-green Macaws (*Ara chloroptera*).

Breeding Macaws

If by the concept of "breeding" you were to understand the planned and directed stabilization, strengthening, or new combination of traits with effects on the next generation in captivity, then this definition would certainly apply to certain species and genera of the order of parrots. In particular, budgerigars (*Melopsittacus*), cockatiels (*Nymphicus*), lovebirds (*Agapornis*), and grass parrots (*Neophema*) would be named, which show their tendency toward domestication above all through the mutations that have turned up.

The animal keeper, however, is inclined to describe as breeding every propagation of the animals in his care, whereby he is wrong in the opinion that this is the best confirmation for optimal keeping and diet, which thus needs no improvement or evaluation. He often leaves out of consideration the great importance of the instinctive necessity for preserving the species.

In my opinion, this concept does not apply to the macaw breedings that have been documented thus far, especially since the few successes have been, to a large degree, of an accidental nature.

Nevertheless, there are various ways in which the interested parrot fancier can change conditions to improve the chances of successful captive propagations.

A Red-and-green Macaw (*Ara chloroptera*) preens the feathers on its shoulder.

Pairing Macaws

One of the most difficult problems in the propagation of large parrots is the putting together of a compatible pair. Distinguishing the sex of parrots lacking sexual dimorphism, to which all of the highly evolved species including the macaws belong, time and again causes even experienced bird keepers difficulty.

Under certain circumstances, however, slight differences in coloration between the sexes exist. The male may be more richly marked and the differently colored areas of the plumage be more distinctly demarcated than in females. In addition, a bird with a large, heavy build along with a flat, "angular" head and heavy bill can be considered a cock in most cases, whereas the build of a hen is slightly more delicate and the head smaller and slightly rounded in profile.

Different fanciers believe that they can distinguish the sexes of their macaws on the basis of the shape of the bill. This is considerably more hooked in the female than in the male, and therefore appears almost as a semicircle in profile. Another, in the meantime frequently practiced method of sex determination is the so-called endoscopic examination, which can be performed by various veterinary specialists as well as at schools of veterinary medicine.

The bird to be examined is first anesthetized, and then a small incision is made beneath the last rib, through which an endoscope can be inserted into the animal's abdominal cavity. A device of this kind normally has a diameter of 2 to 2.7 millimeters and permits—with the aid of a tiny light—the inspection of the abdominal cavity. Using this method the male testes can be precisely distinguished from the female ovaries, and active sex organs from nonfunctional ones. This instrument is also useful for the identification of internal organ diseases, for instance, pathological changes of the lung, such as with tuberculosis or aspergillosis, as well as diseases of the liver and kidneys.

This technique has been tested in the United States for a number of years, and in Germany too it is finding more and more supporters and practitioners. It has also been available to and affordable for the general public for a long time. The dependability of the method is beyond dispute. Only a very small percentage (less than one percent) of the birds that were examined died, and virtually all of these deaths could be traced back to the improper treatment of the birds

Facing page: A group of Scarlet (*Ara macao*) and Blue-and-yellow (*A. ararauna*) macaws.

Below: Macaw hybrids combine traits of both parents; these are the progeny of Red-and-green x Blue-and-yellow macaws (*Ara chloroptera x ararauna*).

after the operation (see Ingram, 1982).

With the development of this method of examination, the veterinarian has finally been given an opportunity for precise sex determination of parrots; however, it must also be pointed out that all members of the highly evolved parrot family Psittacidae are very fussy in mate selection. Birds that have been paired together randomly, which possibly exhibit differences in regard to age, condition, and acclimation, often require many years before egg laying or the successful rearing of young occurs. Despite such difficulty, a modest increase in successful breedings of large parrots has been recorded since the advent of endoscopy.

For the sake of completeness, however, two further methods of sex determination will be described:

The first procedure involves the examination under a microscope of a single feather, which is plucked from the bird of unknown sex. This procedure was developed at the Houston Zoo, Texas, and was used there between 1974 and 1976.

In the second method, developed by biologists at the San Diego Zoo, the sex is determined through the examination of the droppings: the hormone content (estrogen and testosterone) provides information on the sex of the bird.

Neither of these two methods has gained acceptance on a wide scale, especially since purchasing the necessary technical instruments is very expensive and large margins for error apparently must be calculated in.

I have been informed by Prof. Dr. E. Curio, Ruhr University, Bochum, that he has been working on a method of sex determination based on the examination of chromosomes of the blood. At the moment they are working with the blood of cranes and will try to make

Sexing macaws by assessing the slight differences in head shape has proved unreliable. A Blue-and-yellow Macaw (*Ara ararauna*).

Left: Depending on the choice of companions available, a macaw may or may not select a mate of its own species. Here, a Military Macaw (*Ara militaris*) preens a Hyacinth (*Anodorhynchus hyacinthinus*).

this so far costly method affordable for private fanciers in the future.

By far the most promising method, despite the advances in modern scientific techniques, is to permit the birds free choice in mate selection. For this purpose it is best to purchase four to six birds of a species and to keep them together in a large flight. The birds will occasionally pair off at an age of two to three years; however, pairing generally occurs at the onset of sexual maturity with a mate that seems to be suitable.

Such a partnership is seldom characterized by serious problems and usually lasts a lifetime. Feather-plucking adults, interrupted breeding activities, abandoned or killed young, among other things, rarely occur with pairs of this kind—in contrast to ones which have been put together at random. A separation from the "chosen" mate can scarcely be observed with parrots in captivity, unless it does

not satisfy its biological role. If a bird dies prematurely, the remaining bird will find a new mate after a "period of mourning." Unfortunately, the described method is very expensive and assumes the availability of a fairly large flight installation, so that it seems practical only for few fanciers.

Below: For endoscopic sexing, the parrot is anesthetized shortly before the procedure. Sex determination is unproblematical, provided there are no internal abnormalities.

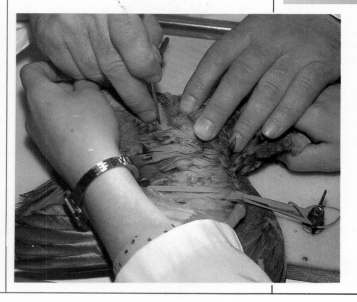

Other Requirements

In addition to determining the sex, other important factors influence whether the captive propagation of macaws will be feasible or not. Above all, the age of the birds is decisive. Unfortunately, the age of birds of unknown provenance can be determined only with great difficulty.

Youngsters are distinguished from subadult or adult birds principally by the dark iris ring. In addition, they often exhibit a smaller size as well as dull plumage colors, together with areas of color that are indistinctly separated from one another. The bill of young parrots is often smooth and shiny; in fairly old birds, on the other hand, it has thin, layered horn laminae, which give the bill an irregular external appearance.

The age at which macaws reach sexual maturity is not precisely known yet, especially since the exact age of a bird at the time of purchase is not usually known. It is suspected that large macaw species become sexually mature at five to seven years of age; in smaller spaces this apparently occurs at three to four years of age. These values should, however, only be considered as rough guidelines and can vary under less than optimal conditions.

The time at which the greater feathers are molted also plays a role in breeding attempts that should not be underestimated. Breeding birds must be fully acclimated and will only be able to incubate and rear young successfully when they are finished molting.

In captivity this can be achieved by keeping breeding birds (this of course does not apply to newly imported birds) at relatively low temperatures (approximately 10 to 15° C) in winter. In this way the birds are not exposed to fairly large temperature variations when they are moved from the indoor space to the outdoor flight; the opposite takes place in late fall, when they go back indoors. When macaws are kept in this way, they start courting when the weather turns warmer (in April in Central Europe; the eggs are then usually laid the

In the Walsrode bird park, the Hyacinth Macaws (*Anodorhynchus hyacinthinus*) first laid eggs in 1982. For Hyacinths, the nest box must have an interior diameter of about sixty centimeters to accommodate the parents and the young.

stimulation for the birds, it is advisable to reduce the size of the entrance hole before breeding begins by nailing on softwood branches. These will be gnawed to pieces by the birds within a short time and will serve to increase the breeding drive. In the lower third of the box, about 10 centimeters above the bottom, a latchable control opening is installed, which permits the interior of the box to be inspected from time to time without having to drive the incubating bird from the nest at the same time. Nevertheless, you should avoid constant inspections, so as to avoid disrupting incubation. It must be

following month).

After each brood the used nest box should be cleaned and disinfected. The tree cavities available in the wild are on average smaller than is generally assumed. In captivity, as well, nest trunks with a diameter of 25 to 50 centimeters and a height of 80 to 100 centimeters are large enough for the larger species; smaller species prefer correspondingly smaller nesting facilities. The entrance hole should be located in the upper third of the nest box and must exhibit, depending on the species, a diameter of 10 to 20 centimeters.

In order to provide additional

Differences in the rate of development are evident in these two Blue-and-yellow (*Ara ararauna*) youngsters, both about ten weeks old.

Right: A group of Red-fronted Macaws (*Ara rubrogenys*) have retreated to the wire roof of their enclosure.

decided from case to case whether a nest-box inspection can be justified without endangering the brood.

The nest box is usually installed in the roofed-in part of the outdoor flight high under the roof of the aviary. Some breeders and zoos report, however, that the larger species sometimes prefer nesting facilities placed on the floor.

The hybrids of *Ara ararauna* and *Ara chloroptera* bred in the Wuppertal Zoo all came into the world in a box made of boards standing on the floor; in contrast, the Red-fronted Macaws (*Ara rubrogenys*) which also breed there clearly favor nesting facilities installed high above the floor (Dr. Schürer, personal correspondence).

Macaws, like these Red-and-greens (*Ara chloroptera*), alter their nesting sites to their taste by gnawing.

The plastic or sheet-metal drums that some macaw keepers use as nesting facilities are unsuitable for a number of reasons.

The young hatch at about the start of June and, depending on the species, are jealously guarded and cared for by the parents until the end of September or the start of October. At the end of the nestling period, approximately at the end of August, the adult birds begin to molt their often badly worn plumage, and again exhibit a complete, functional plumage before the start of winter.

Another important prerequisite is, in my opinion, the keeping of macaws in roomy outdoor flights. Although pairs occasionally breed in large cages, fairly large flights offer much better prospects for success. Here the female also has the opportunity to escape from the intensely courting cock during the precopulative phase. Furthermore, this method of keeping also satisfies the large birds' need for exercise.

In conclusion, it should also be pointed out that as a rule only birds in satisfactory health, which are fed a varied diet and are given optimal accommodations and care, will breed in captivity. Newly imported birds often need many years to become adjusted to the local climate, food, and space conditions.

Preparations for Breeding

In the same way as in the wild, where the food supply of macaws is subject to seasonal change, and in captivity as well, the diet should be varied several weeks before breeding begins. Fruit, sprouted food, and prescribed special rearing food should be offered to the birds, and will serve to stimulate the birds, as does a small, supplemental dose of vitamins (particularly vitamins E and B). Allowing the adult birds to become adjusted to the rearing food in time can be of decisive importance in the subsequent feeding of the young.

Like most representatives of the order Psittaciformes, macaws are also cavity nesters. The white color of the eggs and the long period of development of the young make it necessary in the wild for macaws to camouflage their nests by using hollow tree trunks and niches in cliffs. As a rule, the birds do not excavate their own nest chambers, but instead use available hollow spaces, which, if necessary, are enlarged before breeding begins. A notable exception perhaps, the Red-and-green Macaws (*Ara chloroptera*) were observed in southern Brazil attempting to excavate a nest cavity in a cliff by using their powerful

Three Blue-and-yellow x Red-and-green macaw hybrids were reared in 1981 by Herr Amme of Bissendorf.

bills.

In captivity, nest boxes made of hardwood boards or hollow natural tree trunks are suitable for breeding attempts. In my opinion, natural trunks offer better prospects for success, since the side walls and bottom as a rule consist of rotting

Above: The Red-fronted Macaw (*Ara rubrogenys*) prefers to nest high up in the aviary.

Right: Nestlings of the Red-and-green Macaw (*Ara chloroptera*), just feathering in.

wood, and the moisture content facilitates the subsequent hatching of the young. Furthermore, the eggs during incubation are optimally supported and cannot roll around.

Similar conditions can be simulated in nest boxes constructed of boards by covering the bottom with pieces of rotting wood, which can be found everywhere in forests. In addition, it is advisable to spray the outside of such a box frequently with water, in order to create a reservoir of moisture in the wood. Under certain circumstances, large parrots are very choosy in the selection of the nesting facilities. It is therefore a good idea to install several nest cavities of different

construction in different places within the aviary. Once the pair has selected a box, the remaining ones can be removed. Once chosen, the nest box will be used year after year.

The Course of Breeding

Acclimated, sexually mature macaws in captivity normally begin preparing to breed at the beginning of April. A pronounced courtship behavior—such as we are familiar with in other species of birds—is not observed; however, those behavior patterns that reveal the close social bond between the birds are displayed more frequently.

First and foremost is social grooming, which only occasionally occurs outside of the breeding season and, under certain circumstances, between birds of the same sex. At the same time, both birds display an increased interest in the nest box, the entrance hole and interior of which are now gnawed intensively. The wood shavings produced in the process fall to the bottom of the nest box and form the nesting substrate.

For the first time, courtship feeding can be observed; as a rule, the cock feeds the hen with predigested food from its crop and thereby tests its subsequent function as provider for the female and young. Should the macaw pair still happen to be housed with conspecifics at this time, these should be moved to other flights without delay so that the pair can have its own territory.

In addition, visitors should temporarily not be permitted to enter the aviary installation; the birds also must not be disturbed by activity in and around the bird house or by unfamiliar events,

objects, and noises. The birds now behave very aggressively toward the keeper and other "intruders"; the spectrum ranges from weak willingness to defend the territory up to direct attack.

Mating is the final link in the precopulative phase; its frequency increases just before the eggs are laid. Several copulations a day are

Above: A Red-fronted Macaw (*Ara rubrogenys*) and a Red-fronted Conure (*Aratinga wagleri*) occupy the same accommodations.

Below: A Blue-and-yellow Macaw (*Ara ararauna*) uses its bill to climb onto a post.

Captive-bred Yellow-collared Macaws (*Ara auricollis*): ten, twelve, and fifteen days old (*above*) and four weeks old (*below*).

Yellow-collared Macaw chicks: about five weeks old (*above*) and eight weeks old (*below*).

A look into the nest of Illiger's Macaw (*Ara maracana*). The chicks are between ten and sixteen days old.

the rule.

Egg laying takes place about three to four weeks after the start of the courtship period; the clutch consists of two, more rarely of three or four eggs, which the female lays at intervals of two to four days.

After an incubation period of 24 to 28 days (depending on the species), the young hatch in order according to the intervals in which the eggs were laid. In the first few days, they are fed exclusively by the mother, which takes the predigested formula from its mate's crop and, after digesting it a second time, finally feeds it to the young. After two to three weeks, the cock also takes part in feeding. The food given to the young becomes coarser in consistency over the course of the nestling period.

After 12 to 14 weeks (in small macaws, eight to ten weeks) have passed, the fully feathered young leave the nest box, but must still be cared for by the parents for a fairly long time before they become independent.

Artificial Incubation and Hand-rearing

The rearing of young does not always proceed as "rectilinearly" as was described above. Often the breeder experiences the bitter disappointment that eggs or freshly hatched young are abandoned by the parents. The reasons for this can be manifold, and it is therefore difficult to give universally valid advice here. Frequent disturbance of the breeding pair, inappropriate food (in older young, the quantity of food also plays an important role), unfavorable climate in the breeding space, among other things, can be the reasons. The keeper would do well to scrutinize his keeping conditions from case to case.

Eggs that are not incubated by the adults can be brought to development in a normal incubator at a temperature of 38.5° C and a humidity of 70 to 80 percent. The eggs should be turned twice a day and should occasionally cool down for a short time. Just before hatching, the humidity should, if possible, be increased to make it easier for the young to break through the egg shell.

After hatching, the young still nourish themselves from their yolk supply for several more hours. Artificial rearing should therefore not be started until 10 to 12 hours later. It should also be pointed out that the keeper who decides to hand-rear parrots will be very busy with his charges for a fairly long period of time. Larger macaw species often do not reach independence until an age of three to four months, and during this time—particularly in the first weeks of life—require virtually uninterrupted care.

With the aid of a plastic syringe (without the needle), an easy-to-digest, watery formula, which should be at least lukewarm, is trickled into the bills of the young birds at intervals of two to three hours (except for the nighttime

hours from 10:00 p.m. to 6:00 a.m.) during the first 25 to 30 days. It can be clearly seen through the thin, pink skin of the unfeathered little birds how the formula collects in the crop. At each feeding the bird should only receive so much food so that the crop does not become overfilled. With increasing age and weight, which should be checked

An eyedropper is used to hand-feed a chick of the Yellow-collared Macaw (*Ara auricollis*).

Summary of the Weights of Three Hand-reared Hybrid Macaws for the First Seventy Days of Life

Day	"Mike"	"Pipifax"	"Pan"
1	25 g	26 g	26 g
5	25 g	—	25 g
10	27 g	36 g	29 g
15	36 g	49 g	37 g
20	43 g	61 g	47 g
25	59 g	79 g	52 g
30	70 g	100 g	69 g
40	118 g	130 g	130 g
50	185 g	232 g	215 g
60	260 g	330 g	285 g
70		400 g	370 g

Above: A Blue-and-yellow Macaw (*Ara ararauna*), seven days old.

Left: Development of the young in the Blue-and-yellow Macaw (based on information from H. Linn, Radevormwald). Clutch of two eggs (*top*). The first egg laid measured 45 x 34 mm. (*middle*). Weighing a two-day-old chick (*bottom*).

Below: A Blue-and-yellow Macaw at ten weeks of age.

Summary of Breeding—Biology Data

	Overall Length	Clutch Size	Incubation Days	Nestling Period in Days	Egg Size
Genus: *Anodorhynchus* (3 Species)					
hyacinthinus	100 cm	2–3 (5)	29 (?)		
glaucus	72 cm			120	
leari	75 cm				57.0 x 38.4 mm
Genus: *Cyanopsitta* (1 Species)					
spixii	56 cm	3			34.9 x 28.7 mm
Genus: *Ara* (13 Species)					
ararauna	86 cm	2–3	25	90	46.4 x 35.9 mm
glaucogularis	85 cm				
militaris	70 cm	2–(3)		75–90	46.4 x 32.8 mm
ambigua	85 cm	2–3	23(?)–26	80–90	55.0 x 46.0 mm
macao	85 cm	2–3	25–28	80–104	47.0 x 33.9 mm
chloroptera	90 cm	2–3	26–28	100	50.0 x 35.4 mm
rubrogenys	60 cm	3			
auricollis	38 cm	3		65	
severa	46 cm	2–(3)	28(?)	65–70	38.4 x 30.4 mm
manilata	50 cm				
maracana	43 cm	2	24–27	60	37.1 x 29.9 mm
couloni	41 cm				
nobilis	30 cm	3–4	24	60	32.6 x 24.5 mm

Top: Recently hatched Blue-and-yellow Macaws (*Ara ararauna*), one and three days old. *Middle:* At five and seven days of age. *Bottom:* Two weeks old.

daily, the dietary components must become thicker.

A study by Haas (1977) serves as a guide to keepers for the increase in weight in large macaws; Haas's study involved a hybrid of *Ara ararauna* and *Ara chloroptera*. These birds were artificially reared; they were fed the following formula, which was used successfully in the San Diego Zoo on many occasions: The food consisted of a half cup of wheat groats, two egg whites, and two tablespoons of evaporated milk, which was mixed to a soupy consistency with water and was cooked over low heat until the pap took on a firm consistency. Before feeding, cottage cheese and banana were added, so that the food then consisted of one-eighth cottage cheese, one-eighth banana, and three-fourths pap. Half-ripe, milky maize and sprouted grain were also added. Vitamin preparations and mineral supplements rounded out the mixture.

After a few weeks, the intervals between meals can be increased, and at the end of the nestling period, it is sufficient to feed the young birds only three times a day with a thick pap, which will be taken from a spoon or even from a bowl. The birds are also given sprouted seed in a separate bowl, which they soon learn to husk. From here, the step to the independent intake of the usual seeds is to be considered minor.

Based on the experiences of several zoos, freshly hatched macaws should initially be kept at a temperature of 32 to 35° C in a container in good air circulation. The youngsters were found to suffer from indigestion if the temperature varied too much. In the course of the period of development, the temperatures are lowered slowly and reach normal room temperature after two to three months.

In addition to the previously mentioned formula, human baby food, which can be obtained in any grocery store, and which usually must be mixed with milk or water, can be used as a basic component of the rearing food. Depending on the age of the bird, the consistency of the pap is changed and is supplemented with vitamins, minerals, fruit juices, and finely chopped egg or greenfood.

Macaws that are produced in this manner develop into very tame, amiable house pets, which become closely attached to their keeper. With timely intervention, youngsters that are hatched by the parents and are abandoned by them after several days can also be fed by hand and often will become closely attached to their keeper. In contrast to artificially incubated birds, there is no direct imprinting with these latter birds, so it will still be possible to keep them with conspecifics in the future. In any case, it is extremely difficult for a bird that is attached to humans, much less one that is falsely imprinted on them, to live with a group of normally developed conspecifics.

Life Expectancy

Although wondrous stories have been told about the ages attained by different parrots in the past, documentation that can withstand scrutiny is unfortunately still lacking. Like many other birds and mammals, if macaws are given good

Top: The Blue-and-yellow Macaw chicks at seven weeks of age. *Middle:* At eight weeks. *Bottom:* At eleven weeks, in the nest box.

Above: A hybrid of the Scarlet (*Ara macao*) and the Blue-and-yellow (*A. ararauna*) macaws. This cross has sometimes been called the "Catalina" Macaw.

care in captivity they can live longer than in the wild. Such a bird has neither to search for food nor protect or defend itself against enemies; the risk of falling victim to an accident is also extremely small.

Whereas an age of over 80 years can be substantiated for some cockatoos, macaws—just as amazon parrots—do not appear to live much longer than 35 years. The cases described in the literature in which macaws attained a greater age are to be considered as exceptions.

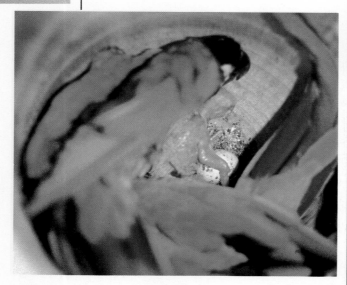

Left and below: In recent years the Yellow-collared Macaw (*Ara auricollis*) has bred many times for private parrot keepers, as well as in the Walsrode bird park. The youngsters shown here at three points in their development are among the twenty-seven macaws of this species which have been produced at Walsrode.

Various stages in the development of the Scarlet Macaw (*Ara macao*, after Müller-Bierl, 1983): thirty-two days old (*top*); thirty-five days (*middle*); thirty-eight days (*bottom*).

Right, top: A wild-caught Red-and-green Macaw (*Ara chloroptera*) with a misshapen bill. *Middle:* Chicks of Illiger's Macaw (*Ara ararauna*) being weighed at 20–25 days of age. *Bottom:* Hand-reared macaw chicks placed in a basket to have their picture taken.

Left, below: Development of the Scarlet Macaw: At 38 days of age (*upper*). After leaving the nest, the youngster, between its parents, is completely feathered and almost indistinguishable from the adults (*lower*).

Red-and-green
Macaws (*Ara
chloroptera*).

Above: A Blue-and-yellow Macaw (*Ara ararauna*) alights on an outstretched arm.

Left and below: Like other energetic young animals, this Blue-and-yellow Macaw enjoys chewing things.

Above: A group of macaws—Military, Blue-and-yellow, and Scarlet—on display in a shop.

Left: As the Blue-throated Macaw (*Ara glaucogularis*) is rare in captivity, breeding has seldom occurred.

The Species of Macaws

For parrot fanciers, the largest parrot in the world, the Hyacinth Macaw (*Anodorhynchus hyacinthinus*), seems to possess a special magnetism.

Genus: *Anodorhynchus* (Spix) 1824

The macaw genus *Anodorhynchus* consists of three species with predominantly blue coloration of the plumage, the total length of which ranges from 72 to 100 centimeters. Common to all species is the bare eye ring as well as the unfeathered area at the base of the lower mandible, while the cheek region—in contrast to *Ara*—is fully feathered.

The extinct species *Anodorhynchus purpurascens* is generally included in the genus *Anodorhynchus*, although the existence of this species, which on the basis of old travel reports occurred on Guadeloupe, cannot be confirmed beyond doubt.

1. Hyacinth Macaw
Anodorhynchus hyacinthinus (Latham) 1790

Description: Total length 100 centimeters; ground color of plumage cobalt blue, darker on the wings; underside of tail gray; unfeathered eye ring and unfeathered area at the base of the lower mandible yellow; bill gray black; iris dark brown; feet dark gray. Juveniles: As adult birds, but with shorter tails.

Range: Southern Brazil in Pará, Bahia, Goias, Minas Gerais, and Mato Grosso.

Life in the wild: Because of its very difficult–to–reach living space in the interior of Brazil, there are scarcely any observations of the Hyacinth Macaw in the wild. In many parts of its range it is a common bird, which favors swampy forests and palm groves as a biotope. It lives in clans of two to 20 birds, whereby the close bond between the pairs is obvious.

Hyacinth Macaws apparently use natural tree cavities (in old palms) as nesting sites, which as a rule are located near watercourses. In addition to fruits, berries, and seeds, its diet consists primarily of large hard palm nuts and the fruits of fig trees.

Keeping: With a total length of 100 centimeters, the Hyacinth Macaw is the largest parrot in the world. Its powerful bill is exceeded in size only by that of the Indonesian–Australian Palm Cockatoo (*Prosciger aterrimus*).

The accommodations for such a majestic bird must consist of a roomy outdoor aviary with a heatable security house. For the

Among Hyacinth Macaws, the close bonding between members of a pair is conspicuous.

breeder who keeps the birds in pairs, a flight space at least six meters long is necessary. The usual aviary wire mesh with a thickness of 1.75 to 2.05 millimeters will withstand the strong bills of the parrots for only a short time. Instead of this, I recommend the use of "wavy" wire mesh with a mesh size of 25 × 25 millimeters or 50 × 50 millimeters and a wire thickness of from four to five millimeters.

In addition, if its wings have been trimmed, the Hyacinth Macaw can also be kept on a climbing tree during the summer. In Birdland, Great Britain, the gradual acclimation to liberty was accomplished in this way. According to de Grahl (1974),

several pairs have been kept there for years at liberty without the birds ever having gone astray or wandering away. Bedford (1957), on the other hand, on the basis of his own negative experiences, does not consider the Hyacinth Macaw to be sedentary. The first Hyacinth Macaw apparently arrived at the London Zoo in 1867. In 1880 it was exhibited by the Berlin Zoo as well as Hagenbeck in Hamburg and other zoos. In subsequent years, it seldom reached Europe.

Since 1970, the Hyacinth Macaw has occasionally been offered by wholesalers—at a high price, however. It is seen more and more frequently in various zoos, bird parks, and with private fanciers, who look upon it, to quote Russ (1882), "actually as a valuable signboard" and beyond that, covet it because of its pleasant temperament.

Its mimicking ability clearly does not match that of the other large macaws; however, it exhibits an extremely playful, amiable temperament toward its trusted keeper.

The Hyacinth Macaw collection of the Bochum Zoo seems noteworthy to me. Five pairs are kept there in a huge flight and can be observed by visitors without the obtrusive wire mesh, since one side of the aviary is glassed in.

In Parrot Jungle, Miami, Florida, in addition to Blue-and-yellow, Scarlet, and Red-and-green Macaws, Hyacinth Macaws prove to be very teachable birds, which can be taught various tricks (Teitler, 1979).

In contrast to two other species *Anodorhynchus glaucus* and

A. hyacinthinus

Anodorhynchus leari, which for years have ranked among the parrot species most threatened with extinction and which are listed in Appendix I of CITES, so far there does not appear to be any immediate threat to the Hyacinth Macaw.

Breeding: Considering the sporadic importation of this species, breeding has succeeded relatively often. The probable first captive propagation occurred in the Kobe Zoo, Japan. In the same year, eggs were also laid in the Chicago Zoo, Illinois. The clutch consisted of five (!) eggs, from which only one chick hatched. Unfortunately, it was not reared by the parents.

A similar fate was suffered by a youngster hatched in 1969 in the Bratislava Zoo, Czechoslovakia, which only survived for two weeks.

Not until 1978 was a second clutch recorded with this pair.

A detailed breeding description was supplied by R. Small, who succeeded in hand-rearing a Hyacinth Macaw in 1971 in the Brookfield Zoo, Chicago (cited from Low, 1980): At the time the first eggs were laid, the female was almost nineteen years old and the male was about thirteen years old. After several infertile clutches between 1968 and 1970, the first breeding success occurred in 1971. Two eggs were laid at intervals of two days and were incubated by the female for 29 days. After hatching, however, the youngsters had to be taken from the nest box for hand-rearing, since they were not cared for by the parents. The young that hatched in the years 1972 and 1973 met with a similar fate.

In flight as well, pairs of Hyacinth Macaws (*Anodorhynchus hyacinthinus*) keep close together.

135

As a prelude to breeding, Hyacinth Macaw pairs engage in mutual preening.

According to Decoteau (1982), the breeding of Hyacinth Macaws has succeeded repeatedly with private breeders in the United States. Besides various natural broods, a fancier from Ohio, who did not wish to be identified, succeeded more than once in rearing young after hatching. As rearing foods he used a mixture of shelled, pulverized sunflower seeds, oatmeal, grated carrot, and vitamin and mineral supplements, which was mixed with water and warmed before feeding. Based on statements from this breeder, the total period of development of the hand-reared young was considerably shorter (?) than with naturally reared young.

In the Federal Republic of Germany, Hyacinth Macaws laid eggs in the Walsrode bird park in 1981 (Robiller and Trogisch, 1982b). In April the female laid a single egg, which, however, on the second nest inspection was found to be broken. So far a second clutch has not been laid. The birds were housed in an aviary with the dimensions of 6 x 1 2.5 x 1 2.5

meters; the nest cavity had an inside diameter of 40 centimeters and a height of 80 centimeters; the diameter of the entrance hole was 12 centimeters.

The behavior of the adult birds just before the eggs were laid was noteworthy. As soon as the macaws heard the keeper approaching, the female disappeared into the nest box without a sound, while the male clung over the entrance hole, so as to protect the entrance.

Once the egg was laid in the box, both birds exhibited different behavior. When disturbed, both disappeared into the nest cavity, and inside the nest the male performed threatening swaying head movements in front of the entrance hole and in this way showed

Developmental Weight of Two Hand-reared Hyacinth Macaws

Age	Weight A	Weight B
Hatching Weight	18.6 g	
14 Days	156 g	189 g
21 Days	302 g	347 g
28 Days	464 g	533 g
35 Days	659 g	668 g
42 Days	643 g (?)	—

readiness to defend the nest.

Also noteworthy is the change in coloration of the unfeathered head area in the female just before egg laying. The yellow-orange-colored eye ring and the area at the base of the lower mandible turned a pale yellowish color for a fairly long time.

A grove of buriti palms in Bahia, Brazil, is typical of the places in which Hyacinth Macaws (*Anodorhynchus hyacinthinus*) occur.

Hybrid breedings: Since 1965 two hybrid pairs of *Anodorhynchus hyacinthinus* and *Ara ararauna* as well as *Anodorhynchus hyacinthinus* and *Ara macao* have been breeding in a bird park in Salt Lake City, Utah. The young from the former mating resemble the Hyacinth Macaw in size and stature, but exhibit a yellow-colored underside (Low, 1980).

2. Glaucous Macaw
Anodorhynchus glaucus (Vieillot) 1816

Description: Total length 72 centimeters; ground color of plumage bluish green, more greenish on the underside; head and nape with greenish gray tinge; throat dark gray brown; upper side

Facing page and left: Hyacinth Macaws (*Anodorhynchus hyacinthinus*).

Below: A Hyacinth Macaw in front of its nest cavity in Bahia, Brazil. These large birds frequently use crevices in the rock outcroppings for nesting.

Hyacinth Macaws (*Anodorhynchus hyacinthinus*) at the entrance to their nesting log threaten the observer. The gnawing around the rim of the hole is typical.

of tail bluish green; underside of tail dark gray; unfeathered eye ring yellow; unfeathered area at the base of the lower mandible whitish yellow; bill gray black; iris dark brown; feet dark gray. Juveniles: have not been described so far.

Range: Paraguay, northeastern Argentina and northwestern Uruguay; formerly also in extreme southeastern Brazil.

Life in the wild: The Glaucous Macaw is an extremely rare bird, which has already been extirpated in parts of its original range. Because of its difficult–to–reach biotope, no detailed publications exist on the habits of this species. The last observations in the wild were apparently made around 1960 in northeastern Argentina, where it favors forests and palm groves as a habitat.

Decoteau (1982) discusses the existence of a small remnant population in Uruguay, while Low (1982) considers the species to be extinct.

Keeping: In the last century the Glaucous Macaw was kept in various European zoos. According to Russ (1882), it reached the London Zoo in 1860, Amsterdam in 1868, and Hagenbeck in Hamburg in 1878. The only references to captive keeping in recent times are found in Decoteau. The author reports on an anonymous European fancier who owns a pair of these blue macaws. The diet of these birds consists of a mixture of turkey rearing food, cottage cheese, and small seeds; the components are stirred to a pap with hot water, which is then offered to the birds freshly prepared twice a day.

Breeding: In past years the aforementioned fancier's pair incubated and reared a fairly large number of young on their own; the breeder hopes to be able to build up a healthy stock with these birds. The nestling period lasted 120 days (!) with each brood.

3. Lear's Macaw
Anodorhynchus leari (Bonaparte) 1856
Description: Total length 75 centimeters; head, nape, breast, and belly region bluish green; feathers in belly region with light tips; back,

A. glaucus

wings, and upper side of tail cobalt blue; underside of tail dark gray; unfeathered eye ring yellow; unfeathered area at the base of the lower mandible light yellow; bill gray black; iris dark brown; feet dark gray. Juveniles: have not been described so far.

Subspecies: The systematic position of Lear's Macaw is disputed; some authors consider it to be a subspecies of *Anodorhynchus glaucus*; others maintain that it is a hybrid of *Anodorhynchus hyacinthinus* and *Anodorhynchus glaucus*.

Forshaw (1973) grants this blue macaw the status of an independent species, whereby he stresses the close relationship to *glaucus*. He considers both species to be distinct

Glaucous Macaw (*Anodorhynchus glaucus*). The rarity of this macaw is such that no photos are available.

from *hyacinthinus*, however.

Range: The species is known only from the border area between Pernambuco and Bahia in northeastern Brazil (Sick, 1960). No further range data are available.

Life in the wild: Observations of Lear's Macaw in the wild have scarcely been managed so far. After several years of searching, the German-born ornithologist Helmut Sick, together with his student Dante M. Teixeira, discovered a small flock of this rare species in 1977/1978 in a difficult–to–reach conservation area in eastern Brazil (Raso de Catarina, northeastern Bahia). About 20 birds were sighted.

As proof of the finding of this "mysterious" macaw species, one specimen had to be shot, which now (as the first bird taken from the wild) enriches the collection of skins of the Museu Nacional, Rio de Janeiro, Brazil (Sick, 1979a, 1979b, 1980, 1982/83; Sick and Teixeira, 1980; Hoppe, 1983).

For the solution of this "greatest mystery in South American ornithology (not only Brazil)" (Sick, by letter), Professor Sick received the gold medal from Brazil at the First Ibero-American Ornithological Congress in Buenos Aires. In order to prevent the animal trade from learning the exact area of distribution and wiping out the newly discovered population, the borders of the conservation area, which has existed since 1975, were expanded by the Secretaria do Meio Ambiente. In addition, SEMA hired a warden whose job is to guard the newly discovered macaw population (Sick, 1982/83).

Keeping: In the past, Lear's

Macaw was occasionally confused with the Hyacinth Macaw. It can, however, be clearly differentiated from it on the basis of plumage coloration and size. This blue macaw is of no importance at all for the parrot fancier, especially since it reaches Europe only extremely rarely (accidentally) as single specimens in shipments of Hyacinth Macaws. If such a bird happens to reach the market, as a rule it changes hands for astronomic (five figure) sums.

Formerly, Lear's Macaw was often found in zoos. For example, it reached London in 1880, Berlin in 1883, and Hamburg in 1893 (de Grahl, 1974). Sick (1960) also calls this macaw a "smaller copy of the

A Lear's Macaw (*Anodorhynchus leari*) at the entrance to its nesting cavity, photographed by a breeder in Brazil.

Hyacinth Macaw, which is exhibited alive in almost all of the larger zoos in the world."

At the moment, however, these rare macaws are still found in only a few collections outside of their Brazilian homeland, where they are carefully tended and are guarded treasures.

Single birds or pairs are found in Birdland, Great Britain; in the San Diego Zoo, California; in Parrot Jungle, Miami, Florida; in Busch Gardens, Tampa, Florida; as well as in the Walsrode bird park in the Federal Republic of Germany. Decoteau (1982) reports on a total of 11 birds (including the specimens in San Diego, Miami, and Tampa), that are being kept in the United States. The existence of additional birds in Europe or elsewhere cannot be ruled out.

Breeding: The probable first captive propagation of Lear's Macaw occurred in July, 1982, in Busch Gardens, Tampa. The male was on loan from Parrot Jungle, Miami. Immediately after hatching, the youngster was brought to Miami and hand-reared there by Mr. and Mrs. Sheer, the owners of Parrot Jungle. In September of the same year, a second chick hatched from a further clutch and was reared by the parents.

A Lear's Macaw (*Anodorhynchus leari*) in the collection of San Diego Zoo.

A. leari

Left: A Lear's Macaw on display in a zoo. It is deplorable that such a rare animal is kept singly, restrained by a chain.

Right: In the Amersfoort Zoo, this Lear's Macaw became bonded with a Blue-and-yellow Macaw (*Ara ararauna*). Subsequently it was sent to the Walsrode bird park in the hope of breeding it.

Facing page: The Spix's Macaw (*Cyanopsitta spixii*) is the only species in the genus. Many systematists consider it to be a transitional form between the genera *Anodorhynchus* and *Ara*.

Genus: *Cyanopsitta* (Bonaparte) 1854

This genus consists of a single species with predominantly blue coloration of the plumage. With the exception of the lores and eye ring, the facial area is—in contrast to the genus *Ara*—completely feathered. Systematists have different opinions on the taxonomic classification of this species. Von Boetticher (1964) classifies it with the macaws of the genus *Ara*, whereas Forshaw (1973) and Wolters (1975) grant it the status of its own genus. The species has been threatened with extinction for years and is protected under CITES.

1. Spix's Macaw

Cyanopsitta spixii (Wagler) 1832

Description: Total length 56 centimeters; ground color of plumage cobalt blue, darker on the back, wings, and upper side of tail; forehead and ear region gray with a blue tinge; crown and nape blue gray; greenish suffusion in belly and breast areas; underside of tail dark gray; unfeathered lores and eye ring black; bill gray black; iris yellow; feet dark gray. Juveniles: Ground color of plumage darker than in adult birds; shorter tail, bill gray black with horn-colored areas on the upper mandible.

Subspecies: None.

Range: Eastern Brazil, in the provinces of Piaui and Parnaguá.

Life in the wild: So far there have been scarcely any observations of the rare Spix's Macaw in the wild. This species was discovered in 1820 by Dr. Spix on a research expedition to eastern Brazil; it was not until 1903, almost a hundred years later, that Reiser (cited from Forshaw, 1973) again sighted a few specimens in the province of Parnaguá, Brazil. It seems to favor palm groves as a living space.

Keeping: Only a few specimens of this extremely rare macaw species are found in captivity outside of their Brazilian homeland. The first specimen reached the London Zoo in 1878; two additional birds lived around 1927 in the Paignton Zoo, Great Britain.

In the United States, Karl Plath obtained a youngster in 1928, which was kept with trimmed wings on a climbing tree. It had considerable mimicking ability and could reproduce several words and short

C. spixii

A young Spix's Macaw (*Cyanopsitta spixii*) photographed in a private parrot collection in Singapore. The dark iris and the light area on the bill identify this bird as a juvenile.

sentences distinctly. At the moment, Spix's Macaws are probably found in Europe only in the Walsrode bird park, in the Naples Zoo, and with an anonymous Belgian fancier.

The Walsrode bird park was able to purchase two youngsters in 1975, which still had to be fed by hand for two months. In 1978 the male died during courtship. Not until the end of 1982 was it again possible to form a new pair. The English veterinarian George A. Smith, Petersborough, who had a single tame bird at his disposal, sent his bird to the park in Walsrode on loan for breeding purposes (Robiller and Trogisch, 1982).

The former Yugoslavian president, Josip Tito, had four Spix's Macaws in his private collection. Unfortunately, nothing is known of the whereabouts of his birds.

According to Decoteau (1982), one pair of this macaw species lives in Belgium and at least three pairs live in the United States, all of which are breeding successfully. Two birds were sold in Great Britain in 1979, which were offered at a price of the equivalent of 22,000 Deutsche marks apiece.

Breeding: Decoteau discusses the successful captive propagation of the Spix's Macaw in Belgium, the Federal Republic of Germany, and in the United States. Unfortunately, he gives no further details.

The pair owned by the Belgian fancier he mentions (whose name he refuses to divulge for reasons of security) has reared a total of 18 young in the last six years (between 1976 and 1981).

Genus: *Ara* (Lacépède) 1799

The genus *Ara* consists of 13 living representatives, whose total length varies between 30 centimeters (*Ara nobilis*) and 90 centimeters (*Ara chloroptera*).

Common to all is the generally unfeathered or only sparsely feathered cheek skin and the long, tapered tail. The former distribution of the genus on the islands of the West Indies is beyond question; with the exception of the Cuban Macaw (*Ara tricolor*), however, it is not absolutely certain whether or not these representatives were identical to living species. The extinct "forms" commonly cited cannot be safely authenticated.

1. Blue-and-yellow Macaw

Ara ararauna (Linné) 1758

Description: Total length 86 centimeters; upper side and uppertail coverts medium blue; forehead and crown olive green; whitish cheek skin with several rows of small greenish black feathers; neck black with greenish colored margin; ear region, sides of neck, and rest of underside of body orange yellow; undersides of tail

Blue-and-yellow Macaws. The large areas of bare cheek skin, usually with lines of small feathers, is characteristic of the genus *Ara*.

The Blue-and-yellow Macaw, *Ara ararauna*, occurs throughout much of tropical South America.

and wings olive gold; bill gray black; iris yellow; feet dark gray; claws black. Juveniles: More washed out in all colors; form smaller; dark iris; light bill, which turns dark after about 15 days (Linn, 1978).

Subspecies: The most recent systematics do not recognize any subspecies of *Ara ararauna*.

The disputed "form" *Ara glaucogularis* was sometimes considered to be a subspecies of the Blue-and-yellow Macaw; on the basis of recent scientific research, however, which compared external appearance, behavior, and calls, the validity of the Blue-throated Macaw as an independent species can no longer be questioned (see Ingels, et al, 1981; Reinhard, 1982).

Range: From eastern Panama to Ecuador and possibly northern Peru; eastern Venezuela, mainly south of the Orinoco, to Guyana and the Island of Trinidad; south through Brazil to Bolivia, Paraguay, and probably northern Argentina.

Life in the wild: Blue-and-yellow Macaws inhabit forests in the immediate vicinity of river courses or swampy areas overgrown with palms. In a certain sense, they can be considered as partial migrants, whose habitat is governed by the available food supply; distances of up to 25 kilometers between roosting and feeding sites have been documented.

The birds are always encountered in pairs; even when they gather in fairly large flocks outside of the breeding season, the pairs fly close together and reveal the close bond between them. The fairly large macaw families have fixed roosting sites, which they leave together

A. ararauna

early in the morning in search of food. All birds of a flock gradually rise into the air and fly with loud screeching over the treetops to their favored feeding areas. They return each evening just before sundown. Their flight is direct and, despite the smooth, slow wing beats, very fast.

The macaws feed on fruits, berries, nuts, and green plants of all kinds, whereby they clearly give preference to the fruits of various palm species (above all the genera *Mauritia*, *Oreodoxa*, *Astrocaryum*, *Bactris*, and *Maximilianea*). In addition, the seeds of a spurge (*Hura crepitans*) were found in the crops of a number of birds.

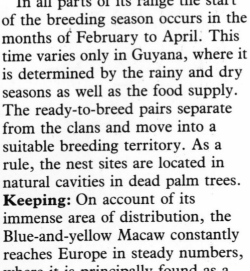

As a candidate for hand-taming, the Blue-and-yellow Macaw is highly desirable, as it has a reputation for a friendly disposition.

In all parts of its range the start of the breeding season occurs in the months of February to April. This time varies only in Guyana, where it is determined by the rainy and dry seasons as well as the food supply. The ready-to-breed pairs separate from the clans and move into a suitable breeding territory. As a rule, the nest sites are located in natural cavities in dead palm trees.

Keeping: On account of its immense area of distribution, the Blue-and-yellow Macaw constantly reaches Europe in steady numbers, where it is principally found as a show bird in zoos, or occasionally with private fanciers. The birds often reach the importers in a half-tame state. They are quite hardy and resilient birds, which survive easily the strain of legal quarantine and generally experience little difficulty in acclimation.

When kept singly, the Blue-and-yellow Macaw—particularly as a young bird—usually quickly becomes tame and closely attached to its keeper. Its amiable temperament, its confidence, and not least, its magnificent appearance, allow it to become a coveted house pet, demanding untiring patience and constant attention from its owner in order to become a well-adjusted creature. A fancier who decides to keep the bird singly, certainly a questionable venture for reasons of species preservation, should become familiar with the situation and keep in mind the permanent responsibilities associated with it. Such a bird is certainly not suitable as the "last word" in interior architecture or an agent of exotic flair.

The mimicking ability of this macaw is considerable, though it falls short of the African Grey. De Grahl (1974) reports a bird that could reproduce 60 words and sentences. Other cases are documented in literature.

Keeping this species permanently in a cage cannot be recommended because of the insufficient opportunity for movement. After the period of acclimation, which can take place in an indoor aviary, it is advisable to keep the bird on an open perch in the house, or on a climbing tree in the garden in good weather. It is advisable in most

Rainforest in the
Rio Napo region
of eastern
Ecuador, at the
edge of the range
of the Blue-and-
yellow Macaw,
Ara ararauna.

cases to limit the bird's full flying ability temporarily by trimming the wings to prevent escape. Any obstruction of its ability to fly will be noticed immediately by the bird and after several futile attempts it will no longer make an effort to leave the climbing tree.

Breeding birds need a roomy aviary, which should be constructed of materials that can stand up to the strong bills of large parrots. The food bowls must be made of unbreakable material or should be permanently installed. If placed on the bottom, unsecured clay bowls will be destroyed by the birds in no time. The main perches should be made of hardwood to withstand the birds' bills for a good amount of

time. It is also advisable to offer a variety of softwood branches (fruit tree, willow) satisfy the birds' need to gnaw and which counter any occurring boredom.

Breeding: The majority of breeding successes have undoubtedly been achieved with this species. In older literature, there are references to successful breedings in the years 1833 and 1892 (France); 1894 (Belgium); 1901 (Czechoslovakia); 1934 (Germany, Gruga Essen); 1934 (Great Britain); and various others.

More recently, as well, reports on various captive breeding successes have been published. Risdon (1965), Kirchhofer (1973), and Linn (1978) successfully propagated the Blue-

and-yellow Macaw. I have also been informed by letter and telephone of further notable and partial successes, which are not mentioned in the literature.

On the strength of all reports, Blue-and-yellow Macaws start breeding at six to seven years of age. Hollowed-out tree trunks, wooden wine casks, or simple wooden boxes are used as nesting facilities, which are placed in the interior space of the aviary. A substrate of rotten wood has proven effective with most breeders and provides optimal support for the eggs.

As a rule, the clutch consists of two, or more rarely, three eggs, which exhibit an average size of 46.4 × 35.9 millimeters (Schönwetter, 1964). They are incubated solely by the female, while the cock crouches next to the hen in the nest or stands guard before the entrance hole. The young hatch after an incubation period averaging 25 days; according to de

Grahl (1974), they are only sparsely covered with down and weigh 30 grams immediately after hatching. Linn (1978) describes the young hatched by his birds as completely bare after hatching, without down. The upper and lower mandibles were initially light-horn-colored and slowly turned darker after the 15th day of life. On the 25th day, the first feather sheaths appeared; six weeks later, the birds were fully feathered and exhibited weights of 1125 grams and 1075 grams. After a total nestling period of three months, the young left the nest box and became independent after an additional three weeks.

According to Risdon and Linn, young Blue-and-yellow Macaws at an age of six weeks differ from the adult birds only in the dark color of the eyes.

The temporary pink-red color in the cheek region of the Blue-and-yellow Macaw, which in the past was often considered to be a sex-

Facing page: Perhaps surprisingly, some individuals of the large macaw species, like this Blue-and-yellow, have shown themselves to be very gentle with children. However, owners should take care to supervise all interactions between children and parrots.

Only small macaws are suited to continual confinement in a cage or indoor aviary. Typically, the large species, such as this Blue-and-yellow Macaw, *Ara ararauna*, need a spacious flight.

specific characteristic or an indicator for the onset of sexual maturity, seems noteworthy. In the meantime, however, both of these theories have turned out to be wrong. According to my own observations, hens as well as cocks, which had been endoscoped, occasionally exhibit this peculiarity; it cannot be used as a characteristic for distinguishing the sexes.

This phenomenon apparently does not signal the onset of sexual maturity or the breeding drive either, since youngsters bred by Kirchhofer exhibited the described coloration of the cheek skin immediately after leaving the nest.

The majority of fanciers who have succeeded in breeding the Blue-and-yellow Macaw had a roomy aviary with an attached, heatable security house at their disposal.

Hybrid breedings: Different macaw species occasionally hybridize in captivity. This can frequently be observed in zoos where several species of the richly colored birds are kept in the same display aviary, where, for lack of a suitable member of the same species, birds often have no choice but to choose a mate of a different species.

Dr. Vogt informs me (personal correspondence) of a successful cross between a Blue-and-yellow Macaw and a Scarlet Macaw in the Krefelder Zoo. In 1973, the birds reared two young in a fairly large community aviary, which represented a mixed product between both foundation species with regard to plumage coloration.

The married couple G. and O. Amme, Bissendorf, reported a hybrid breeding between a Blue-

and-yellow Macaw and a Red-and-green Macaw in the year 1981 (see Heemann, 1983). Apparently the most prolific hybrid pair—consisting of a Blue-and-yellow Macaw and a Red-and-green Macaw—is owned by the Wuppertal Zoo. Numerous young have been bred and in part hand-

the birds and brought to development in an incubator (temperature 37.8° C, humidity 65%). The young macaws hatched after 25 and 26 days; they had pecked at the egg about 24 hours before. At an average egg weight of 30 grams, the hatching weight of the young was between 25 and 26

The parent macaws, a Red-and-green and a Blue-and-yellow, produced three youngsters of the same size and coloration.

reared there since 1963.

A detailed description of the courtship, incubation, and rearing of the young is found in Haas (1977): In the outdoor parrot enclosure two birds of the two species mated in 1961. Already in June of 1963 a fertile clutch of three eggs was laid, which was taken from

grams. The keeping temperature after hatching was 33 to 34° C. The young parrots received a diet of cooked pap, which was fed to them six times a day between 6:00 a.m. and 8:00 p.m. The birds' development was complete after a total of five months; they did not become independent, however,

This look into the nest box of Blue-and-yellow Macaws reveals a seven-week-old youngster and an infertile or addled egg.

until the seventh month of life.

Since 1964 the macaws in the Wuppertal Zoo have incubated their own eggs and also care for the young until they become independent. In the meantime, a total of about 40 hybrids are now found there, which are completely identical with respect to plumage coloration and markings. Based on the knowledge gained so far, it can be assumed that intermediate inheritance exists in a crossing of the Blue-and-yellow Macaw and a Red-and-green Macaw species. In the meantime, several of these hybrids have mated with one another and have laid eggs; however, so far all clutches have proved to be incapable of

development (Bock, oral communication).

In Switzerland, the crossing of a Red-and-green Macaw and a Blue-and-yellow Macaw also succeeded with M. Meier in Horgen in 1982 (see Handschin, 1982). The name "Paradise Macaw" proposed by Meier (by letter) cannot, however, be uncritically adopted here. Even though a breeding success with large macaws is seldom managed, it should also not be forgotten that, in this case, it is a question of a hybrid breeding, the value of which for preserving the species is questionable. Giving such hybrids a new name seems confusing to me—at least for the beginner.

Low (1980) reports on an

intergeneric mating of *Ara ararauna* × *Anodorhynchus hyacinthinus* in a bird park in the United States.

2. Blue-throated Macaw

formerly: Candinde Macaw
Ara glaucogularis (Dabbene) 1921
formerly: *Ara caninde*

Description: Total length 85 centimeters; upper side including the front of the head and forehead bluish green (in clear contrast to the medium blue of the Blue-and-yellow Macaw); cheek area smaller than in *ararauna* and with rows of closely spaced, dark-green feathers; throat spot dark blue; underside orange yellow to reddish yellow (Reinhard, 1982); undersides of wings orange yellow; upper side of tail blue; underside of tail olive yellow; bill

In markings and hue, these two hybrids (*Ara ararauna* x *A. chloroptera*) in the Bretten Bird Park provide an interesting contrast with a normally colored *ararauna* individual, shown above.

Two Blue-and-yellow Macaws, *Ara ararauna*. Among captive macaws, mutual preening is a favored occupation.

gray black; feet dark gray.

Subspecies: Up to the beginning of the 1970s, the Blue-throated Macaw was still occasionally classified as a subspecies of the Blue-and-yellow Macaw (de Grahl, 1974; Low, 1982).

At present, noted ornithologists advocate the view that *glaucogularis* must be an independent species (Forshaw, 1973; Ingels, et al, 1981; Wolters, 1975). Dr. R. Burkard, Baar, Switzerland, who has kept two pairs of this species for a long time, informs me by letter that on the basis of coloration, bill shape, nature of the rows of feathers on the cheeks, calls, as well as the overlapping ranges, with *glaucogularis* it can only be a question of an independent species (clearly distinct from *ararauna*).

Reinhard (1982) also refers to the differences in the calls of both species: in the same situations the Blue-throated Macaw screeches at a higher pitch than does the Blue-and-yellow Macaw. Furthermore, he mentions the museum skins of *ararauna* and *glaucogularis* (in the Carnegie Museum, Pittsburgh, Pennsylvania) studied by Forshaw, which unequivocally come from the same region in Bolivia (District of Buenavista) and which prove that, at least in parts of their areas of distribution, both forms occur sympatrically. Zoogeographically, the sympatric distribution of closely related forms without recognizable intermediate forms argues in favor of the existence of species, not subspecies.

Range: Bolivia (District of Buenavista), Paraguay, and northern Argentina. Based on the current data of Ridgley (1980), the living space of the Blue-throated Macaw is located in Bolivia, near the town of Trinidad.

Keeping: Experiences in the keeping of the Blue-throated Macaw exist only to a very limited extent, especially since importations must be described as extremely rare.

In the Federal Republic of Germany, to my knowledge, this species is found only in the Walsrode bird park and in the Berlin Zoo, where an endoscoped pair is being kept at present. In addition, Dr. R. Burkard,

For a long while the systematic status of the Blue-throated Macaw, *Ara glaucogularis,* was unclear. Now, however, all taxonomists agree that it is a separate species.

A. glaucogularis

Switzerland, has two pairs (communicated by letter) as does Mr. Kiessling in Tenerife. The existence of other Blue-throated Macaws in Europe cannot be ruled out, especially since birds of this species were offered for sale in 1982 in the advertisement section of a relevant specialist journal.

R. Reinhard, Berlin Zoo, informed me of details on the keeping of the Blue-throated Macaw, of which the zoo has a total of three specimens. During the period of acclimation the birds were considerably more sensitive than Blue-and-yellow Macaws. The adjustment to the new environment

and diet took longer than with other macaws, an experience that was confirmed by a South American exporter. His freshly caught Blue-throated Macaws overcame their initial unruly temperament considerably later than the Blue-and-yellow Macaws caught at the same time. After acclimation they no longer differ from other macaw species in regard to diet and care.

Breeding: So far, apparently only the South African breeder Gill du Venage, Transvaal, has succeeded in breeding the Blue-throated Macaw. In the last three years, his birds have reared four young (Hayward, 1983).

3. Military Macaw
Ara militaris (Linné) 1766

Description of the nominate form: Total length 70 centimeters; ground color of plumage green with olive suffusion on the back and wings; head lighter green than the remaining parts with a bluish frosting on the occiput; forehead red; flesh-colored cheek skin with several rows of small greenish black feathers; throat spot olive-brown; rump feathers and back light blue; greater wing coverts light blue; upper side of tail red brown, with a bluish tinge in places; undersides of tail and wings olive yellow; bill gray black; iris yellow; feet brown black. Juveniles: In all colors duller.

Subspecies: Forshaw recognizes three subspecies with geographically isolated ranges. They differ slightly from one another in size and coloration.

1. *Ara militaris militaris* (Linné)
Range: Tropical zones from Colombia as far as the northwestern part of Venezuela; south as far as eastern Ecuador and northern Peru.

2. *Ara militaris mexicana* (Ridgway)

Description: Resembles the nominate form, except larger.

Range: Mexico, with the exception of the rainforest zones.

3. *Ara militaris boliviana* (Reichenow)

Description: As *militaris*, except the throat spot is red brown; feathers in the ear region with a reddish tinge.

Range: Tropical zones of Bolivia and extreme northwestern Argentina.

Life in the wild: The Military Macaw principally inhabits dry forests and open scrubland in arid zones; it also occurs on mountain slopes near the coast and in pine and oak forests up to an elevation of 2500 meters. As a rule, it avoids the tropical rainforest; its ecological role is taken over there by the Scarlet Macaw (*Ara macao*). In parts of its habitat, it is still common; however, its numbers—in the same way as with other species of large macaws—have definitely decreased in extensive areas because of shooting and the collecting of young.

Military Macaws are migrants whose habitat at any given time is governed by the available food supply. They leave their roosting places just after sunrise in flocks of 10 to 30 birds to go in search of food together.

Besides various seeds, buds, and berries, they appear to give preference to the fruits of fig trees.

The breeding season occurs—depending on the area of distribution—between March and June. The nest is located in a dead-tree cavity (apparently *Pinus*

Military Macaw, probably the nominate form *Ara militaris militaris*, which is found in Colombia, Venezuela, Ecuador, and Peru.

species). Fleming and Baker (cited from Forshaw, 1973) give an account of woodcutters who found a macaw nest in a tree that contained two broken eggs. The nest chamber, which had originally been excavated by woodpeckers, had an inside diameter of 33 centimeters and was located at a height of about 20 meters above the ground. The nesting substrate consisted of coarse wood shavings.

Keeping: The Military Macaw is seldom encountered in fanciers' homes or in zoos. According to Decoteau (1982), Military Macaws make good house pets; they have an extremely pleasant, amiable temperament and a good mimicking ability. In addition, because of their teachability, they are occasionally trained by artists for circus performances.

As aviary birds, Military Macaws need a large flight space with an

A. militaris militaris

attached security house; neither wood nor other "soft" material may be used in the construction, since these macaws rank among the worst "gnawers" within their genus.

The utterances of this species surpass by far those of the other large macaw species; therefore, breeding pairs may only be kept permanently in outdoor aviaries in rural areas. In densely populated regions, it is advisable—in consideration of the neighbors—to allow the birds to stay in the

outdoor aviary only by the hour.

Finally, the experiences of Russ (1882) with this macaw species are repeated in the following: "At present it is seen now and then in bird shops and at exhibitions; all of the prominent zoos have it, and it proves to be very persistent there, for in Frankfurt a Military Macaw lived roughly fifteen years. In the Hamburg Zoo, ones perches unchained on the rod, and it does not have the least intention of leaving the same. At wholesale dealers the macaw with the red forehead is found in an unusual diversity of sizes, and the systematists have therefore separated it into two species. This is of no significance to the fancy, however; if worse comes to worst, you can buy a Great Green or Military Macaw according to taste."

Breeding: The Military Macaw has rarely been propagated in captivity so far. In 1963, young of this macaw species were successfully reared in the Wellington Zoo, New Zealand; in 1964 in the Fort Worth Zoo, Texas; in 1974 and 1975 in the East Berlin Zoo, Democratic Republic of Germany; in 1978 in Busch Gardens, Florida; as well as with P. V. Springmann in Texas. In addition, Decoteau (1982) names other fanciers in the United States who recorded breeding successes in past years.

The clutch consists as a rule of two, or more rarely, three eggs, which exhibit an average size of 46.4 × 32.8 millimeters. The precise incubation period has not been determined yet; however, it probably amounts to 25 to 27 days. The fully feathered young Military Macaws leave the nest cavity at an

A. militaris mexicana

age of 11 to 14 weeks.

Hybrid breedings: Hybrids between the Scarlet Macaw and the Military Macaw, as well as between the Red-and-green Macaw and the Military Macaw, have been produced in the past in various zoos and bird parks.

4. Great Green Macaw

Ara ambigua (Bechstein) 1811

Description of the nominate form: Total length 85 centimeters; ground color of the plumage green, similar to *Ara militaris*, but lighter with a yellowish tinge; forehead scarlet; lower back and tips of the uppertail coverts light blue; upper region of the tail coverts reddish brown; undersides of tail and wings olive yellow; rows of black feathers in the otherwise unfeathered, whitish cheek region; bill gray, turning lighter toward the tip; iris yellow; feet gray. Juveniles: In all colors duller; tail feathers edged dull yellow; iris brown.

Subspecies: Systematists recognize

A. militaris boliviana

two races of *Ara ambigua*, which differ only negligibly from each other.

1. *Ara ambigua ambigua* (Bechstein)

Range: From Nicaragua through Costa Rica and Panama to western Colombia.

2. *Ara ambigua guayaquilensis* (Chapman)

Description: Resembles the nominate form; bill smaller than in *ambigua*; undersides of tail and wings greenish.

Range: Western Ecuador and possibly southwestern Colombia; the areas of distribution of both subspecies apparently do not overlap.

Beside the Red-and-green Macaw is a Military Macaw of the nominate subspecies *militaris*.

A Military Macaw, *Ara militaris*, cracking a sunflower seed, one of the dietary staples for macaws in captivity.

Life in the wild: As a living space the Great Green Macaw favors forests in the tropics and subtropics up to an elevation of 650 meters above sea level. In contrast to former times, today it is only rarely found near human settlements. In northeastern Nicaragua as well as in Costa Rica, its range overlaps that of the Scarlet Macaw (*Ara macao*).

The Great Green Macaw is encountered in pairs, clans, or small flocks of up to twelve birds. Its diet consists of fruits, berries, nuts, seeds, buds, and green plants.

Keeping: The Great Green Macaw is occasionally mistaken for its smaller relative, *Ara militaris*. However, it differs from that species in size as well as in the green coloration of the plumage. This is clearly lighter in the back region and on the nape in *Ara ambigua* than in *Ara militaris*.

Great Green Macaws are encountered even much more rarely than the Military Macaw in zoos and bird parks, and with private fanciers. The few imported birds as a rule quickly find a fancier and often change hands for a "handsome" price.

As a house pet, this macaw ranks with the most intelligent representatives of its genus, and has the ability to mimic words and noises and, in addition, to learn tricks of many kinds. According to Teitler (1979), it is especially suited for riding acts in circuses.

As early as the end of the last century, the first Great Green Macaw reached the Berlin Zoo. At present, single birds, pairs, or small groups of this species are found in the zoos in East Berlin (German Democratic Republic) and Bochum

The Great Green Macaw, *Ara ambigua,* naturally less widespread than the similarly colored Military, is also much less common in aviculture.

(Federal Republic of Germany), in the Walsrode (Federal Republic of Germany) and Cornwall (Great Britain) bird parks, as well as in other institutions and with a few private fanciers.

Breeding: The probable first captive breeding occurred in 1974 in the East Berlin Zoo. Three young, of which two were reared, were hatched from three eggs; a youngster was successfully reared there in 1975 (Low, 1980).

The first breeding in Great Britain succeeded in 1977 in the Cornwall Bird Paradise (Reynolds, 1977). Between 1974 and 1975 an attempt had been made there to acclimate a pair of Great Green Macaws to liberty. In contrast to other macaw species—which to some extent breed even at liberty—this attempt was unsuccessful and it was decided to trim their birds' flight feathers to prevent the birds

In this photo the difference in size between the Great Green Macaw (*Ara ambigua*) and the Military (*A. militaris*) is evident.

Broadly circulated photographs and other depictions of *Ara macao*, the Scarlet Macaw, have caused it to typify macaws in most people's minds.

from escaping. The macaws were then kept outdoors on a large climbing tree.

Two eggs were laid in April of 1976. They were incubated by the parents for 12 days and were then broken. A second clutch laid in August was removed from the nest box immediately as a precaution and was brought to development in an incubator; the young that had hatched died within a few hours.

Another egg was laid in 1977 and was put under an incubating pair of Scarlet Macaws. After an incubation period of 25–26 days the youngster hatched and was reared without difficulty by the "substitute parents." Just before leaving the nest—at an age of ten weeks—the keepers took the youngster from the box and continued to feed it for an additional three weeks until it attained independence.

In the United States, the breeding of the Great Green Macaw appears to have succeeded several times with a veterinarian, who wishes to remain anonymous (Decoteau, 1982).

5. Scarlet Macaw
Ara macao (Linné) 1758
Description: Total length 85 centimeters; ground color of plumage scarlet; back, rump, and uppertail coverts bluish; wing coverts and scapulars yellow with green tips; underwing coverts red; tail feathers scarlet with bluish tips; underside of tail orange to brownish; unfeathered cheek area cream colored, with narrow rows of small red feathers; upper mandible horn-colored, blackish toward the base; lower mandible gray black;

A. ambigua ambigua

A. ambigua guayaquilensis

Though it resembles the Scarlet Macaw, the Red-and-Green Macaw has lines of feathers on its cheeks and lacks yellow on the wings.

iris yellow; feet dark gray.
Juveniles: Lower mandible grayish; iris brown; tail shorter; the green area of the wings can be more extensive in juveniles than in adult birds (Low, 1980).
Subspecies: None.
Range: Oaxaca, Mexico to southern Panama; east of the Andes from Colombia in the north to La Paz, Bolivia in the south; east through Brazil to Guyana and to the island of Trinidad.
Life in the wild: Even today, the Scarlet Macaw is still one of the most frequently encountered South American parrots, although its

numbers have clearly decreased in recent years due to shooting and collecting. Thus, with many authors there are references to decimated or extirpated populations in parts of its former range, for example, in Veracruz, in parts of Mexico, as well as in Guatemala (see Forshaw, 1973).

Lowland rainforests near rivers at elevations of under 1000 meters are its preferred living space, which in some regions overlaps that of the Blue-and-yellow Macaw.

Scarlet Macaws are encountered in pairs, clans, and small flocks of up to 30 birds, whereby the close bond between two mated birds is apparent even in flight. They stay so close together that their flight feathers sometimes touch. The flocks undertake extended flights daily, often showing up in places where particular fruits, nuts, and so forth have attained a preferred degree of ripeness; grain and maize fields are also visited by them, where they often—much to the distress of the owner—cause great damage. The birds spend a large part of each day in the search for food, before returning with loud screeching to their roosting trees at sundown.

As a nest cavity Scarlet Macaws use large tree hollows, which are returned to every year. The resident natives consider these nest sites as family property, which are always passed down to the descendants. Tame parrots, which they take from the nest as youngsters, are always found in the residential areas of the natives. These serve as objects of value in exchange and, in bad times, apparently also as a food reserve. The long tail feathers, which were

regularly pulled out of the birds, formerly were used as decorative objects.

Keeping: Along with the Blue-and-yellow Macaw and the Red-and-green Macaw, the Scarlet Macaw is still among the most common macaw species in captivity. As can

be proved, it already was looked upon as a coveted house pet in the Inca cultures of the Middle Ages.

Just as with these other species, according to Bedford (1954), it is suited for keeping at liberty. In the Metelen and Walsrode bird parks as well as the Wuppertal, Cologne,

Scarlet Macaw in the outdoor exhibit at the Walsrode bird park, which had fifteen macaw species in its collection.

and other zoos, this method of keeping has been practiced for years with good results.

The once-frequently observed practice of chaining birds to a climbing ring is to be avoided for various reasons; in parklike gardens, on the other hand, it is recommended to keep macaws on a large, branched climbing tree, during which—after first trimming the flight feathers—the birds can be adjusted to keeping at liberty.

When kept singly, the Scarlet Macaw displays an amiable disposition and becomes closely attached to its keeper. Its mimicking ability is considerable; however, the words it reproduces are harder to understand than those of the African Grey Parrot. However, according to de Grahl (1973), this species is better suited for keeping in a community aviary than are the closely related Blue-and-yellow and Red-and-green Macaws.

Breeding: The captive propagation of the Scarlet Macaw has been documented in the literature since 1916 (L. H. Chamness, California). Lord Lilfors, Great Britain, was able to achieve further successes between 1934 and 1939; his Scarlet Macaws were kept at liberty at times and reared their young in outdoor nest cavities.

Since then, Scarlet Macaws have been bred successfully in many zoos, bird parks, and with private fanciers. On the reliability of many reports, these macaws assume an extremely aggressive temperament toward their keeper, which surpasses by far the comparable behavior patterns of the Red-and-green and Blue-and-yellow Macaws. Intruders who enter the aviary to inspect the nest cavity are violently attacked, sometimes head-on and chased with open bill.

Generally speaking, Scarlet Macaws lay two, more rarely three or four, eggs, which exhibit an average size of 47 × 33.9 millimeters (Schönwetter, 1964). The female starts incubating immediately after laying the first egg; some breeders suspect that the male also takes an active part in incubation at times. The young hatch after an incubation period that averages 26 days; they are

A. macao

completely bare except for the whitish down. The eyes open between the tenth and twelfth day of life. The first feather sheaths appear after almost four weeks.

In the first days, the young parrots are fed exclusively by the hen, which takes the predigested formula from its mate's crop and then feeds it to the brood. According to Decoteau (1982) and J. Bordiek, Metelen bird park (oral communication), young Scarlet Macaws develop very slowly. They indicate periods of between 90 and 104 days for the nestling period. A further three to four weeks go by before the young can take up food on their own. Like many other parrots, young Scarlet Macaws often weigh more than the parents before leaving the nest box. A few days after leaving the nest, however, their body weight is reduced by about ten percent, so that they attain an average weight of 650 to 800 grams.

Hybrid breedings: Hybrids between the Scarlet Macaw and the Blue-and-yellow Macaw have been produced in the Krefeld Zoo (Dr. Vogt, by letter). In 1973, the birds reared two young in a community aviary, which represented a mixed product of both foundation species with respect to their coloration. In the United States, hybrids of this kind apparently were bred so frequently that they were given the name "Catalina Macaw" (Decoteau, 1982).

In addition, hybrids between Scarlet and Red-and-green Macaws as well as between Scarlet and Military Macaws have been reported (de Grahl, 1974).

Developmental Weights of a Scarlet Macaw (after Muller-Bierl, 1983)	
Age in Days	*Weight in Grams*
10	100
20	390
30	595
40	800
50	810
60	890
70	950
80	890

Long familiar to parrot fanciers as a result of its large range, the Scarlet Macaw nowadays is considered a highly threatened species.

173

6. Red-and-green Macaw

Ara chloroptera (G. R. Gray) 1859

Description: Total length 90 centimeters; ground color of plumage red, darker than in *Ara macao*; median wing coverts, inner secondaries, tertiaries, and shoulders green; lesser wing coverts green; back, rump, uppertail coverts and undertail coverts light blue; greater wing coverts and outer secondaries blue; outer vanes of primaries dark blue; tail dark red with blue tips; undersides of tail and wings dark red; unfeathered cheek region with narrow rows of reddish feathers; upper mandible horn-colored with gray-black coloration at the base; lower mandible gray black; iris light yellow; feet dark gray. Juveniles: Tail shorter than in adults; lower mandible and base of the upper mandible medium gray; iris brown.

Subspecies: None.

Range: From eastern Panama, northwestern Colombia east of the Andes, and Venezuela to Guyana; south as far as the provinces of Paraná and Mato Grosso in Brazil; northeastern Bolivia, Paraguay, and northern Argentina.

Life in the wild: The Red-and-green Macaw is principally a resident of tropical forests in lowlands and foothills. In montane regions, on the other hand, it is encountered more rarely. In the last fifty years, it has withdrawn from the coastal regions more and more into the interior, where, together with the Scarlet Macaw (*Ara macao*), it is reckoned among the most common large parrots. In the extreme south of its range, in the province of Formosa, northern Argentina, it has been sighted only sporadically.

In contrast to other macaws, which frequently live together in fairly large flocks, Red-and-green Macaws are seen only in small clans or in pairs. The nesting habits of this macaw species have not been sufficiently researched in its homeland so far. Like other representatives of the genus, they also apparently nest in tree cavities of dead rainforest giants; in southern Brazil, Red-and-green Macaws were observed trying to excavate nest chambers in rock faces with the aid of their powerful bills.

Keeping: The richly colored Red-and-green Macaws are highly prized

A. chloroptera

With the extensive cutting of rainforest in large parts of South America, the Red-and-green Macaw, *Ara chloroptera,* has been pushed back from the coastal regions of Brazil into the interior.

The Red-and-green Macaw possesses eye-catching plumage. Among some of the indigenous peoples of the Americas, macaw feathers are used in religious ceremonies.

by the natives as house pets; their nest trees are part of the family possessions and are passed down from generation to generation. The attractive tail and flight feathers are plucked from the macaws at regular intervals and serve the owners as decoration and objects of value in exchange.

On account of confusion with the previously discussed Scarlet Macaw, the first importations of this macaw species cannot be documented beyond all doubt; however, the Red-and-green probably came to Europe at the beginning of the seventeenth century. Since then it has been put on the market regularly.

Because of its attractive appearance, the Red-and-green Macaw, along with the Blue-and-yellow and Scarlet Macaws, is part of the usual bird stock in zoos, bird parks, and so forth. On the other

hand, it is encountered considerably less frequently with fanciers.

On the strength of all reports, the Red-and-green Macaw exhibits a less amiable temperament in captivity than its close relative, the Scarlet Macaw. Nevertheless, it can become very tame and confiding toward its keeper. Its mimicking ability is considerable; however, the sounds are reproduced relatively inarticulately. This species does not differ from the other large species of its genus with respect to keeping requirements.

Breeding: The first captive propagation apparently was achieved by J. S. Rigge, Millom, Great Britain, in the year 1962 (Rigge, 1963). The breeder obtained his pair in 1956; four years later the first infertile clutch was laid. In the following year, two young hatched from a further clutch (consisting of three eggs with an average size of 50 × 35.4 millimeters), which, however, lived for only a few hours. In June of 1962, more eggs were laid and about four weeks later two young hatched. The hen left the nest for the first time when the young were almost five weeks old. In the meantime, the female was provided with food by the cock. The young macaws were fully feathered at an age of 60 days. They left the nest box five weeks later.

In the United States, the Red-and-green Macaw was successfully bred by H. I. Gregory, Texas, in 1972. The clutch consisted of three eggs, which all hatched after an incubation period of exactly 27 days. After five weeks the young macaws were no longer fed by their parents and had to be reared by hand. The aviary dimensions were

1.8 × 3.6 × 1.8 meters. A 200-liter sheet-metal barrel with an entrance hole of 25 centimeters in diameter served as a nest box. The nesting substrate consisted of dry wood shavings and shredded branches (Gregory, 1972).

The Hannover Zoo and the Metelen bird park, Federal Republic of Germany, as well as various other zoos and private fanciers throughout the world have also enjoyed breeding successes.

Hybrid breedings: Crosses between the Red-and-green Macaw and the Blue-and-yellow Macaw, the Scarlet Macaw, and the Military Macaw have occurred fairly often. A very "productive" mixed pair is owned by the Wuppertal Zoo. There a Blue-and-yellow Macaw and a Red-and-green Macaw have hatched and, for the most part, also reared close to 40 young in the last 18 years.

Barrels have often been turned into nest boxes for the large macaws: the size is suitable, and the wood takes considerable gnawing.

In bird shows, a Red-and-green Macaw is often one of the performers doing tricks.

Bred by Max Meier in Horgen, Switzerland, this macaw is a hybrid of *Ara ararauna* x *Ara chloroptera*.

7. Red-fronted Macaw

Ara rubrogenys

(Lafresnaye) 1847

Description: Total length 60 centimeters; ground color of plumage olive green; head green; forehead, front part of head, ear spot, and thigh red; carpal edge, bend of wing, and lesser underwing coverts orange red; greater underwing coverts and underside of tail olive yellow; tips of the flight feathers and primary coverts blue gray; upper side of tail olive green, interspersed with blue; unfeathered, pink cheek region with rows of brownish black feathers; bill gray black; iris orange; feet dark gray. Juveniles: Forehead red, no additional red areas of plumage in head region; lesser wing coverts and bend of wing green; lesser underwing coverts orange; thigh green with reddish tinge.

Subspecies: No subspecies are known so far.

Range: Provinces of Cochabamba and Santa Cruz, Bolivia.

Life in the wild: Until the start of the 1960s, the Red-fronted Macaw was thought to be extinct, and was known to the scientific world only through museum specimens. Soon after, however, in an area of only 1000 square kilometers (Low, 1980), ornithologists again discovered a number of specimens that travel in pairs or in groups of up to 12 birds. According to Cordier (cited from de Grahl, 1973), this species inhabits hot, dry valleys, mainly at elevations of about 2000 meters. The nests, which according to the statements of the natives are supposed to consist of thorny branches, are built in crevices.

On account of its lack of mimicking ability, the Red-fronted Macaw is scarcely kept as a house pet by the natives. They do, however, occasionally kill it for its colorful feathers and tasty meat.

Red-fronted Macaw perched at the entrance to its nest.

A. rubrogenys

Keeping: Up until 1973 the Red-fronted Macaw was known only to very few parrot fanciers and was of no significance at all as an aviary bird. At the beginning of 1973 the first specimen apparently reached John Halford, Hampshire, Great Britain (Low, 1980); two additional birds were obtained by Dr. R. Burkhard in Switzerland (de Grahl, 1974). At virtually the same time, the Walsrode bird park obtained several specimens, as did H. K. Pöpping in Münster (oral communication). According to Decoteau (1982), the first specimens did not appear in the United States until 1976, where they were offered at enormous prices.

After further importations, in the meantime Red-fronted Macaws are also found in other bird parks and zoos (for example, in the Wuppertal Zoo and in the Bochum Zoo) and in a few private collections. Even today, this macaw species is occasionally still offered in the advertisement sections of relevant specialist journals; the prices demanded by the wholesale dealers have since clearly fallen, but are still considerably higher than with other species of the genus.

According to one importer, the acclimation of newly imported birds presents certain difficulties. Apparently, the birds become accustomed to seeds and other types of food very slowly; on the other hand, they are scarcely sensitive to cold at first and quickly become acclimated to European climate. Nevertheless, Red-fronted Macaws—as is also true of the remaining species of the genus— require a heated shelter in bad weather.

Based on the experiences of the Birdland, Great Britain, and Walsrode bird parks, these parrots definitely tolerate other conspecifics, so that it was decided to keep several birds in a colony system in those parks.

Breeding: The probable first and so far only breeding of the Red-fronted Macaw in the Federal Republic of Germany succeeded in the Wuppertal Zoo (Dr. Schürer, by letter).

Three youngsters were hatched there in 1978 and were hand-reared by the keeper, M. Bock, immediately after hatching. Eight more birds were hatched and reared independently by this breeding pair between 1979 and 1982. In contrast to that of the adult birds, the red coloration on the head is not present on birds that have just left the nest; it appears during the first few months after departure from the nest. The Red-fronted Macaws are kept in an indoor aviary in the Wuppertal Zoo and use nest boxes of thick boards, which are installed under the aviary's roof.

At a length of about sixty centimeters, the Red-fronted Macaw, *Ara rubrogenys,* is intermediate between the large macaw species and small. It and the Blue-throated are the most endangered macaw species.

A. auricollis

plumage (de Grahl, 1980).

Subspecies: The taxonomic schemes on which these descriptions are based do not recognize any distinguishable subspecies.

Decoteau (1982), however, separates the species into two "types," whereby in addition to the nominate form he recognizes a second, which differs clearly from the first on the basis of its orange-colored nape band. In addition, he describes the ground color of the plumage as brownish green, in contrast to the dark green of the normal yellow-naped form.

Unfortunately, there are no further references in the literature to the existence of this orange-naped macaw named by Decoteau, so that it would be premature to append an additional macaw subspecies to the existing classifications before more detailed research is conducted in the wild.

Range: From Mato Grosso, Brazil, and Bolivia through Paraguay as far as northwestern Argentina.

Life in the wild: So far very few observations of this species in the wild have been reported in the literature. Yellow-collared Macaws seem to be common birds in many parts of their range. They travel in pairs or small flocks. Goodfellow (cited from Forshaw, 1973) observed these parrots in Bolivia near the Itenez River, where they were encountered in large flocks during the dry season. At the beginning of the rainy season they migrated in a southerly direction.

As a living space they apparently favor subtropical forests in the immediate vicinity of water holes.

Keeping: At the beginning of the

8. Yellow-collared Macaw

Ara auricollis (Cassin) 1853

Description: Total length 38 centimeters; ground color of plumage green; forehead, crown, and cheeks brownish black; occiput tinged bluish; yellow collar in nape region; flight feathers and primary coverts blue; upper side of tail blue, brownish toward base; undersides of tail and wings olive yellow; unfeathered cheek region cream colored; bill gray black, horn-colored toward tip; iris orange; feet yellowish. Juveniles: Green color lighter; yellow nape band narrower; yellow speckling of the breast

Only in recent years has the Yellow-collared Macaw, *Ara auricollis,* been more or less available to fanciers. Prior to 1970, it was a great rarity in Europe.

Yellow-collared Macaws have been successfully accommodated in captive conditions and many pairs have gone on to breed successfully.

1970s, the Yellow-collared Macaw was considered to be a great rarity in Europe; at that time specimens of this species apparently were kept in the Federal Republic of Germany only in the Walsrode bird park.

Between 1973 and 1979, however, several large importations reached the market, so that in the meantime, Yellow-collared Macaws can be found in a number of zoos, bird parks, and private collections. Since 1980 individual specimens have been imported only sporadically. These macaws do not differ from other smaller species of the genus with respect to keeping requirements.

In Decoteau there are references to the keeping of the Yellow-collared Macaw at liberty. The owners of the birds live in a rural area near a pine forest. During the summer months, the birds are let out of the aviary each morning. They perch in the large pines at the forest's edge and pull apart the seed-bearing cones. Before nightfall and at the approach of stormy weather, they return willingly to their accommodations, where they are always fed each evening.

Breeding: Not counting a breeding in the United States in 1981 which has not been further documented (Busch Gardens, Tampa, Florida), in the Federal Republic of Germany it has been possible to propagate the Yellow-collared Macaw repeatedly. The first German breeding apparently must be credited to the Walsrode bird park, where in 1976 one youngster was reared (International Zoo Yearbook 1977). In the meantime, a total of 27 youngsters have reached independence there (Trögisch, oral communication).

In 1979, K. Maass, Drensteinfurt, succeeded in rearing three young (see de Grahl, 1980), the dates of development of which could not be determined because of the pronounced territorial defense of the adults. It was possible to distinguish the sexes of the breeding pair by a comparison of the yellow collar. In the male bird it was wider and more intensely colored than in the female.

A detailed breeding report is offered by H. Ploog, Seedorf, who had a successful breeding in 1981 (Ploog, 1982): Four birds were obtained in 1979, whereby—as it later turned out—it was a question of two pairs. One pair took possession of a nest cavity in a natural trunk after a short time and defended it against the other aviary occupants. In the spring of 1981, increased social grooming and courtship feeding were observed. The first clutch was laid in May after prior copulation. Three young

Yellow-collared Macaw housed in an indoor aviary.

hatched and were jealously guarded and defended by the parents. They were completely covered with gray down. Three weeks after hatching, the first feather sheaths appeared; after a further four weeks, the young parrots were completely feathered. They left the nest cavity for the first time after a nestling period of nine weeks, but repeatedly returned to the nest during the day and most always at night. Four weeks after leaving the nest, they were still fed by the parents, which, despite a diverse food supply, offered only parrot food and sprouted sunflower seeds to their brood. A total of more than four months passed before the young attained independence.

9. Chestnut-fronted Macaw
  Ara severa (Linné) 1758
Description of the nominate form: Total length 46 centimeters; ground color of plumage green;

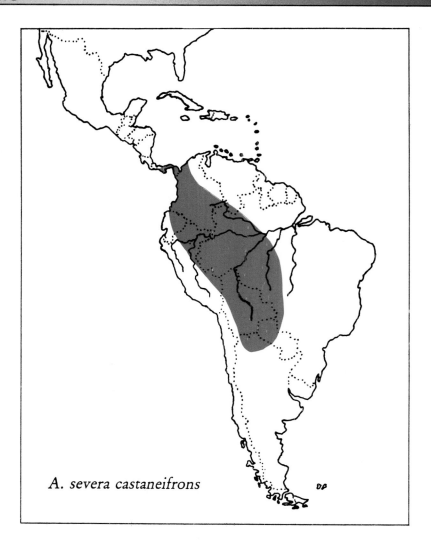

A. severa castaneifrons

crown interspersed with bluish; forehead, chin, and edges of cheeks red brown; unfeathered cheek region cream colored, with tiny rows of small, black feathers; outer vanes of the primaries and primary coverts blue; speculum, bend of wing, and lesser underwing coverts red; greater underwing coverts olive green; tail reddish brown on top, interspersed with green and blue toward tip; underside of tail and underwing coverts orange red; bill gray; iris yellow; feet gray.
Juveniles: In all colors duller; iris black for several months, then whitish yellow; young females, in first year, lack forehead band (de Grahl, 1973).

Subspecies: With this species, all systematists recognize, besides the nominate form, the subspecies *Ara severa castaneifrons*, of which Forshaw (1973), however, entertains doubts about its existence.

1. *Ara severa severa* (Linné)
Range: From the Orinoco region in Venezuela to Guyana in the east; south as far as the Amazonas region in northern Brazil.

2. *Ara severa castaneifrons* (Lafresnaye)

Description: Resembles the nominate form, except larger.

Range: From eastern Panama and western Colombia east as far as the Orinoco region, Venezuela, and south through eastern Peru to northern Bolivia and northwestern Brazil.

Life in the wild: The Chestnut-fronted Macaw is frequently encountered in forests of the tropical regions, preferentially near river courses. It occasionally leaves the true climax forest to visit maize and grain fields in search of food. In addition, wild fruits, berries, and seeds, which are found in the treetops, make up its diet. Preferred fruits are figs, mangoes, and the seeds of the spurge *Hura crepitans*.

Keeping: Chestnut-fronted Macaws are occasionally encountered in zoos and with private fanciers as singly kept birds and as aviary pairs. They are imported sporadically in small numbers and, on account of their pleasant temperament, quickly find a buyer. As a house pet, this small macaw becomes exceedingly tame

and confiding; its mimicking ability is decisively greater than that of its richly colored relatives.

Newly imported Chestnut-fronted Macaws are sensitive to low temperatures at first and must be kept at room temperature; an acclimation to outdoor keeping must take place slowly.

The following passage takes us back to the previous century. Russ

Chestnut-fronted Macaws, *Ara severa*. The size difference between these two birds is not sexual but subspecific: the smaller is the nominate form, the larger *castaneifrons*.

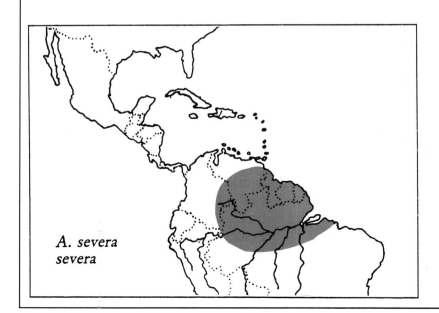

A. severa severa

A Chestnut-fronted Macaw seen from behind. The smaller macaws are less variously colored than the larger species.

(1882) quotes the naturalist Buffon, who reports on his experiences with the Chestnut-fronted Macaw: "Buffon already writes quite fully on its life in captivity. He praises

the small macaw, not only as a beautiful and rare bird, but also because of its gentle, ingratiating temperament; it has the ability to mimic human speech, as well as the screeching and whistling of other birds, and it learns the former more easily and clearly than the large macaws. It listens to other talking parrots and learns from them. However, its voice is not as loud, and it does not pronounce the word 'ara' as clearly as the large species."

Breeding: The world's first planned breeding of the Chestnut-fronted Macaw occurred in 1940 in the San Diego Zoo, California (de Grahl, 1974).

Further breeding successes were achieved in 1954 by O. Hirthe, Copenhagen, Denmark; the Whipsnade Zoo, London, Great Britain, in 1961; H. Kleiser, Hof, Federal Republic of Germany, in 1964; P. Mullick, India, in 1968; and the Cincinnati Zoo in the United States in 1970. Additional unpublished captive propagations are likely.

The pair of Chestnut-fronted Macaws owned by the Dane Otto Hirthe reared a total of nine young between 1954 and 1958. The incubation period could not be precisely determined; it apparently amounted to between 25 and 28 days. At an age of eight weeks, the young parrots left the nest box and they attained their independence six weeks later.

Decoteau (1982), on the other hand, speaks of an incubation period of 28 to 30 days and a nestling period of 70 to 80 days.

Hybrid breedings: A hybrid breeding between the Chestnut-fronted Macaw and Illiger's Macaw was achieved by the German breeder K. Oehler, Friedrichshafen, in the year 1973.

An alert Chestnut-fronted Macaw. Here the red on the carpal edge of the wing can be seen well.

10. Red-bellied Macaw

Ara manilata (Boddaert) 1783

Description: Total length 50 centimeters; ground color of plumage green; underparts and neck, back, rump, uppertail coverts olive green; crown greenish blue; lower cheek region bluish; chin, throat, and upper breast area gray, edged greenish; belly and rump region red brown; feathers of the thigh green with red edging; undertail coverts bluish green; uppertail coverts green with yellow edges; flight feathers, primary coverts, and greater wing coverts dull blue, edged greenish; underwing coverts yellow green; tail green above; undersides of tail and wings olive yellow; unfeathered cheek region yellow; bill gray black; iris dark brown; feet dark gray. Juveniles: No precise data; according to Low (1980), birds that are not yet fully colored possibly exhibit a blackish or brownish feathered head area.

Subspecies: None.

Range: From Guyana through northern and southeastern Venezuela to Colombia, east of the Andes; south as far as northeastern Peru and to the Mato Grosso region in Brazil; Island of Trinidad.

Life in the wild: On the strength of all reports, the Red-bellied Macaw is a common bird in virtually all parts of its range; its numbers appear to be increasing on the island of Trinidad. Its preferred habitat is moist savanna regions with stands of palms, but it can also occasionally be found in agricultural areas. Its occurrence is directly dependent on the distribution of the palm genus *Mauritia*. These macaws were observed by Herklots (cited from Forshaw, 1973) on the island of Trinidad. Their main period of activity began in early afternoon. Together with amazon parrots (*Amazona amazonica*), the birds went in search of food in flocks of more than 100, whereby they gave preference to the fruits of the Mauritia palms.

Red-bellied Macaws nest in cavities of dead palms; during the rainy season the bases of such trees are often under water, which offers effective protection against predators.

Keeping: "The Red-bellied Macaw has not been imported alive so far, although according to Burmeister, Schomburgk, and others it is supposed to be one of the most common parrots of its homeland. It is to be expected, however, that sooner or later it will be brought here in large numbers." (Russ, 1882).

Although at that time Dr. Russ predicted the rapid increase in its availability in Europe in the future, even today it is still found only very sporadically in captivity. Whereas in Great Britain, only singly kept specimens seem to be present, Decoteau (1982) reports on eight authenticated pairs in the United States.

In the Federal Republic of Germany, the Walsrode bird park obtained the first specimen in 1973. In the meantime, additional birds have been imported and—if the advertisements in a relevant specialist journal can be believed—offered at a very favorable price. There are hardly any references in the literature to successful keeping in captivity. J. Halford, Hampshire, Great Britain (cited from Low, 1980), describes his Red-bellied Macaws as delicate birds, which should not be kept in an outdoor flight even in summer. Because of his own negative experiences, he keeps his remaining specimens year 'round in a heated indoor room.

References to dietary peculiarities

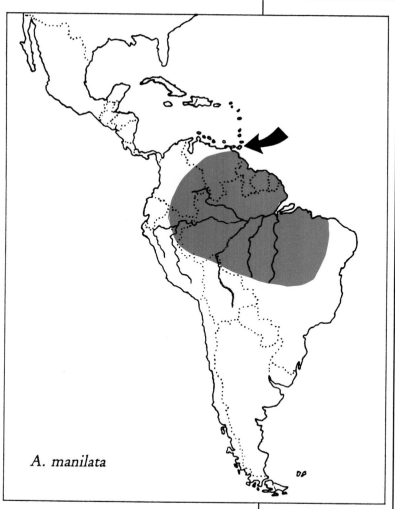

A. manilata

of this macaw species cannot be found in the literature. Dr. Decoteau, Dunstable, informed me by letter that his Red-bellied Macaws are fed in the same way as other small macaw species. Besides the usual seeds, he offers above all apples, pears, bananas, oranges, and papayas. In addition, nuts of all kinds are preferred foods.

Breeding: There are no reports of a successful captive propagation. B. Andrews, Rhode Island, United States (cited from Decoteau, 1982), owned a ready-to-breed pair of birds that was several years old. Unfortunately, the female died of egg binding in 1980.

As the name suggests, red on the abdomen is the most conspicuous plumage feature of this macaw.

In the wild the Red-bellied Macaw is a dietary specialist, feeding almost exclusively on the fruits of the mauritia palm, *Mauritia flexuosa.*

11. Illiger's Macaw

Ara maracana (Vieillot) 1816

Description: Total length 43 centimeters; ground color of plumage green; rump and uppertail coverts olive green; forehead red; head, nape, and cheek region greenish blue; crown blue; spots on back and belly red; primaries and primary coverts blue; secondaries and outer upperwing coverts blue with green edging; bend of wing bluish green; underwing coverts olive green; upper side of tail blue, reddish brown toward tip; undersides of tail and wings olive yellow; unfeathered cheek region light yellow; bill black; iris orange; feet flesh colored. Juveniles: Red color of the forehead paler; spots on belly and back yellowish green; head gray green.

Subspecies: None. I advise the reader, however, to refer to the remarks concerning *Ara couloni* in the section on subspecies.

Range: Eastern Brazil south of the Amazonas, Paraguay, and northeastern Argentina.

Life in the wild: Only meager information exists on Illiger's Macaw's habits in the wild. It inhabits forest regions near rivers or near the coast. The stocks have shown a sharp decrease in many parts of its range. As a result of increasing changes in its original living space (chiefly the cutting of tropical forests near the coast), the species has been forced to withdraw into the interior. This macaw lives in pairs during breeding season. At other times it occurs in small flocks, which in their search for food do not spare maize and grain fields and at times cause great damage there.

In the United States, the Fish and Wildlife Service (Department of the Interior) is considering placing Illiger's Macaw on the list of threatened species and stopping its importation (Decoteau, 1982).

Keeping: In the past, Illiger's Macaws were imported only sporadically, and even then only in small numbers. Nevertheless, they are enjoying increasing popularity among parrot fanciers, especially since they display a pleasant temperament as house pets and as a rule exhibit good mimicking ability.

However, Dr. Russ (1882) had a totally different view of the matter over 100 years ago: "Described and named by Vieillot (1816) and almost as common as the former [meant is the Chestnut-fronted Macaw] on the

Illiger's Macaws, *Ara maracana*. The increasing interest in macaws among bird keepers and breeders has extended to this species as well, with a concomitant revision of its reputation.

A. maracana

market, so far there are no detailed reports of any kind regarding the life in the wild or the behavior in captivity. . . . Since they cause damage to maize fields and at the same time their flesh yields an excellent broth, they are hunted heavily . . . In captivity the bird is just as unpopular as its above-mentioned relative."

If Illiger's Macaw is kept as a breeding bird, it requires a long flight with an attached security house; this must be heated to 10 to 15° C during the winter to prevent colds.

Breeding: The sexes are very difficult to differentiate in *Ara*

maracana; however, in contrast to cocks, hens as a rule exhibit a smaller spot on the belly. In addition, the red coloration in the female's back and forehead region is also less intense and is poorly set off from the surrounding areas of plumage.

In captivity, after courtship and copulation, the hen lays two or three eggs (with an average size of 37.1 × 29.9 millimeters) in April or May, which it incubates for 24 to 26 days. After hatching, the young are covered with white down almost 20 millimeters long. The total nestling period lasts between nine and ten weeks.

The first breedings of Illiger's Macaw were reported by the London Zoo; a total of ten young were hatched there between 1931 and 1938. Further captive propagations succeeded in 1972 in Tropical Bird Garden, Great Britain; in 1973 with E. L. Hauters, Belgium; in 1974 with B. R. Aldred, Great Britain; in 1979 in the Duisburg Zoo, Federal Republic of Germany; as well as in several other institutions and private collections. The American R. Small, Chicago, was the first to hand rear two Illiger's Macaws.

For several years the Duisburg Zoo has owned a pair of Illiger's Macaws, which bred for the first time in 1979. The clutch consisted of two eggs, which were incubated for 24 days exclusively by the female. During this time, the female left the nest very rarely at irregular intervals, in order to feed briefly or to defecate; otherwise, it was fed by the male. The nestling period lasted about nine weeks. After leaving the nest, the young were still fed by

Illiger's Macaws in the collection of the Walsrode bird park. Of the small macaws, only Illiger's has a red front.

View of subtropical deciduous forest in Paraná, Brazil. Such habitat is preferred by Illiger's Macaw, *Ara maracana*, and the Red-shouldered Macaw, *Ara nobilis longipennis*. In locales which only a few years ago were undisturbed, today only remnants of the original forest can be found. The extensive clearing has driven the parrots from their ancestral territories.

both parents for about 60 more days.

From spring until late fall, the breeding pair is kept in an outdoor aviary with the dimensions of 2.5 × 2.5 × 3 meters, in which breeding also takes place. The birds spend the winter in a heated aviary in the zoo's bird house.

A cavity in a natural trunk with a height of 70 centimeters and an inside diameter of 50 centimeters served as a nest box. The diameter of the entrance hole was about 12 centimeters.

It is noteworthy that just before they begin breeding the parents react very sensitively to disturbances (from the keeper) and fight aggressively with each other (Ostenrath, by letter).

F. Veser, Tettnang, apparently owns prolific Illiger's Macaws (see Hoppe, 1982). This breeder's birds reared a total of 53 (!) young from 1974 to the spring of 1982. Since 1976, the macaws have bred twice a year; three eggs are always laid and incubated in both the first and second broods. Captive-bred Illiger's Macaws owned by Mr. Veser already laid fertile eggs at an age of two years.

Hybrid breedings: A cross between a 1,0 Illiger's Macaw and a 0,1 Chestnut-fronted Macaw was accomplished in 1973 by K. Oehler, Friedrichshafen (de Grahl, 1974). After an incubation period of 24 days, the two young hatched and were fed by both parents. They left the nest box at an age of eight weeks and resembled the Chestnut-fronted Macaw in appearance.

12. Blue-headed Macaw
Ara couloni (Sclater) 1876

Description: Total length 41 centimeters; ground color of plumage green; underparts yellowish; head with the exception of the cheek area blue; primaries and primary coverts blue; secondaries and outer upperwing coverts blue with green edging; upper side of tail blue; underside of tail and wings olive yellow; unfeathered cheek region blue gray; bill gray black, horn colored on the tip of the upper mandible; iris yellow; feet flesh colored. Juveniles: Juveniles of this species have not been described so far.

Subspecies: According to the views of leading systematists, the Blue-headed Macaw does not form any subspecies. Taylor (1958), however, considers this species to be a close relative of the Illiger's Macaw, without, however, questioning its validity as an independent species. The analysis of the calls is an important aid in the taxonomic classification of this macaw species and for deciding

A. couloni

Blue-headed Macaw, *Ara couloni.*

whether it is an independent species or a subspecies of Illiger's Macaw; based on observations by O'Neill (1969), the Blue-headed Macaw has a soft, high-pitched voice—in contrast to the harsh, guttural calls of Illiger's Macaw. It therefore seems reasonable to classify them as an independent species. Unfortunately, no comparisons of the behavior of the two species that could support this view have been made yet.

Range: Eastern Peru and apparently the bordering western part of Brazil.

Life in the wild: O'Neill made the only observations so far of the Blue-headed Macaw in the wild in Brazil (cited from Forshaw, 1973). He encountered the macaws at the Curanja River in Balta; the birds lived there in pairs or in small groups of three individuals up to an elevation of 300 meters above sea level. They did not, however, associate with the more common Chestnut-fronted Macaws that also occurred there (*Ara severa*).

Keeping: According to de Grahl (1973), the first Blue-headed Macaw reached the Berlin Zoo in the year 1913; D. West, Great Britain, owned another specimen in 1959.

In the United States, Decoteau (1982) was able to trace a total of four Blue-headed Macaws, which lived with three different owners. Only one of these fanciers at present possesses a sexually mature, endoscoped pair, which, however, does not exhibit any breeding ambitions. Apparently no parrot of this species lives in Europe at the moment. There are no references in the literature to peculiarities in the keeping of the Blue-headed Macaw.

Breeding: The Blue-headed Macaw apparently has not been propagated yet in captivity.

13. Red-shouldered Macaw
Ara nobilis (Linné) 1758

Description of the nominate form: Total length 30 centimeters; ground color of plumage green, underparts yellowish green; forehead and crown blue; bend of wing, speculum, and greater underwing coverts red; outer vane of the outermost primary blue; underside of tail and wings olive yellow; unfeathered cheek region white; bill dark gray; iris orange red; feet dark gray. Juveniles: No blue color on the forehead and crown; bend of wing and speculum green; iris brown.

Subspecies: Three subspecies are generally recognized.

1. *Ara nobilis nobilis* (Linné)
Range: Guyana, eastern Venezuela, and Brazil north of the Amazon.

2. *Ara nobilis cumanensis* (Lichtenstein)
Description: Larger than *Ara nobilis nobilis*; upper mandible horn-colored; lower mandible gray.
Range: Brazil south of the Amazonas in Pará, Maranhão, and Bahia.

3. *Ara nobilis longipennis* (Neumann)
Description: Resembles the race *Ara nobilis cumanensis*, except larger; Forshaw (1973) questions—on the basis of the slight difference in size—the existence of this subspecies and proposes considering *longipennis* to be conspecific with *cumanensis* in the future.
Range: Southern Brazil, Mato Grosso, Minas Gerais, São Paulo, Espírito Santo, and Goiás.
Life in the wild: On the strength of published observations of the

Red-shouldered Macaw in the wild, it is a shy bird in its homeland, which, in some regions, is sedentary and, in others, occurs in accordance with the current food supply. In Guyana it chiefly occurs near the coast, where it is frequently encountered in grain plantations as well as in forests and savanna regions. In Venezuela, on the other hand, its occurrence seems to be dependent on the distribution of various palm species, the fruits of which it relies on.

The macaws travel around in small flocks and at the same time give off loud screeching calls, which apparently help the pairs to stay in close contact and enable the birds to communicate with one another in the air. Red-shouldered Macaws favor cavities in the trunks of palms as nest sites; however, now and then they also build their breeding dwellings in the nests of arboreal termites.

Keeping: The Red-shouldered Macaw is less frequently

At a length of thirty centimeters, the Red-shouldered Macaw, *Ara nobilis,* is the smallest macaw species. Because of its similarity to the *Aratinga* conures, some systematists have placed it in an intermediate genus of its own: *Diopsittaca.*

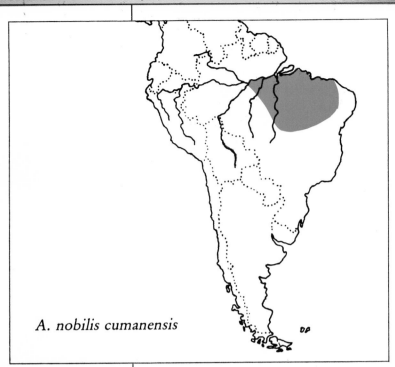

A. nobilis cumanensis

kept at a room temperature of 10 to 15° C in the first winter. Not until the following spring can a gradual acclimation to the outdoor aviary take place. In addition, it is advisable to provide the macaws with a roosting box all year 'round, which they—independent of age and social bonds—seek out at night for protection against cold.

In captivity the Red-shouldered Macaw is a skillful, agile flyer, which despite its "small" stature needs a long flight space. On account of its piercing calls, which are impossible to ignore, it is a good idea—in consideration of the neighbors—to put it in the outdoor flight only at certain times of day. It is not recommended to keep the Red-shouldered Macaw with other species of parrots; however, it is quite possible to keep it in a flock of conspecifics. They act peacefully toward one another and display only weak aggressive tendencies. Even breeding attempts by mated birds within a flock of several birds have not been disrupted by the unmated aviary inhabitants. More than other species of the genus, the Red-shouldered Macaw is prone to feather plucking in captivity.

Because of its appearance, this smallest of all macaws cannot deny its close kinship with the genus *Aratinga*; it is occasionally confused with the Blue-crowned (*Aratinga acuticaudata*). In contrast to *Ara nobilis*, however, the eye ring of [the conure] is completely surrounded by feathers.

Breeding: The captive propagation of the two subspecies *Ara nobilis nobilis* and *Ara nobilis cumanensis* has already succeeded frequently. The first breedings probably

encountered in fanciers' aviaries than are its large, richly colored relatives. Its uniform coloration, as well as its piercing calls, which are produced at all hours of the day, could be reasons for this. In opposition to this, there is the bird's great need to confide, its intelligence, combined with considerable mimicking ability.

Dr. Russ was already aware of this macaw's vocal dexterity over 100 years ago: "In Mrs. P., Vienna, it (the Red-shouldered Macaw) has found a loving keeper, who reports that a pair in her possession is unsurpassed in tameness and amiability and the male could compete with the best Grey Parrot in talking ability . . . . It has learned a total of fifty words, and the way it knows how to use the same correctly is astounding" (Russ, 1882).

Newly imported birds are relatively delicate and should be

occurred around 1940 in the United States; however, which of the subspecies was bred at that time is not known. In 1949, *Ara nobilis cumanensis* was bred—apparently for the first time in Europe—by E. N. T. Vane, Great Britain (Vane, 1950). Four eggs (with an average size of 32.6 × 24.5 millimeters) were laid at intervals of two days and were incubated exclusively by the female. All four fully feathered young left the nest box after 60 days. This pair reared 30 young up to 1956. This subspecies was also bred in 1963 at Birdland, Bourton-on-the-Water, Great Britain (de Grahl, 1975).

The propagation of the nominate form was managed at the start of the 1970s by the Englishman J. Halford, Hampshire, who, in 1972 and 1974, released six birds on each occasion from his own captive-bred stocks on the island of Tobago with the goal of re-establishing the birds, which had been extirpated there (Low, 1980).

A detailed description of his breeding of the nominate form is provided by de Grahl (1975): At the start of 1975 the author obtained four Red-shouldered Macaws, of which two paired off and inspected the available nest box after a four-week-long period of acclimation. The sexes of these two birds were clearly recognizable. Although there were no differences in coloration, the male was distinguished by its more robust, angular head. The size of the unfeathered cheek region was also clearly larger in the male bird than in the female.

An initial infertile clutch (consisting of two eggs) was followed at the beginning of March

A. nobilis nobilis

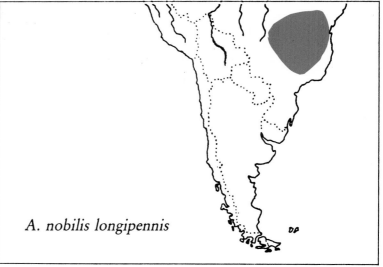

A. nobilis longipennis

of 1975 by a clutch of four eggs, from which one youngster hatched in April. It was taken from the nest for the first time and photographed at an age of ten days; its body was sparsely covered with fine down. After 18 days the eyes began to open

An amicable group of Red-shouldered Macaws, *Ara nobilis.* Conspecifics of this macaw seem to be particularly peaceable toward one another.

and the first feather sheaths were visible under the skin. At an age of five weeks, the youngster weighed 150 grams and one week later, 180 grams. It was almost fully feathered after 55 days. It left the nest cavity a few days later and soon after that

began feeding independently. Despite being offered a varied diet, the parents took only sprouted sunflower seeds for rearing. Only just before the youngster left the nest did they also feed it grated carrot, mixed with egg food.

Red-shouldered Macaw. Sheaths of new feathers are visible on the neck.

Zoological Gardens and Bird Parks

A visit to the zoos listed below can be profitable to the interested parrot lover. Besides the various macaw species, other kinds of parrots will also usually be exhibited.

The listing makes no claim to completeness. Institutions that display only single specimens of the widely seen large macaws (*Ara ararauna, A. macao, A. chloroptera*) have not been included.

Germany
Berlin: Zoologischer Garten
Berlin: Tierpark Berlin-Friedrichsfelde
Bochum: Tierpark
Cologne: Zoological Garden
Geiselwind: Vogel-Pony-Märchen-Park
Metelen: Vogelpark Meteler Heide
Rothenfelde: Vogelpark
Walsrode: Vogelpark
Wuppertal: Zoologischer Garten

Europe and Overseas
Bourton-on-the-Water, England: Birdland
Chester, England: Chester Zoo
Maspalomas, Grand Canary: Palmitos Park
Miami, Florida: Parrot Jungle
Puerto de la Cruz, Tenerife: Loro-Parque
Rode, England: Tropical Bird Gardens
San Diego, California: San Diego Zoo
Wassenaar, The Netherlands: Tiergarten Wassenaar

Bibliography

Arndt, T. 1981. *Keilschwanzsittiche.* Müller-Verlag, Walsrode. [In English as *Encyclopedia of Conures,* T.F.H. Publications.]

Bedford, Duke of. 1954. *Parrots and Parrot-like Birds.* All Pets Books, Fond du Lac.

Boetticher, H. b. 1964. *Papageien.* Ziemsen-Verlag, Wittenberg-Lutherstadt.

Bosch, K. & U. Wedde. 1981. *Amazonen.* Müller-Verlag, Walsrode. [In English as *Encyclopedia of Amazon Parrots,* T.F.H. Publications.]

Brereton, J. & K. Immelmann. 1962. Head-scratching in the Psittaformes. *Ibis* 104, 167–175.

Burkard, R. 1980. Ein weiterer "Rätselara," *Gef. Welt,* 104, 40.

Dabenne, R. 1920. El "Caninde" de Azard es el *Ara ararauna. Hornero* 2, 56.

———. 1921. Algunas palabras más sobre el cambio de nombre del *Ara caninde. Hornero* 2, 225.

Deckert, G. & K. Deckert. 1982. Spielverhalten und Komfortbewegungen beim Grünflügelara. *Bonn. zool. Beitr.* 33, H. 2–4, 269–281.

Decoteau, A. E. 1982. *Handbook of Macaws.* T.F.H. Publications, Neptune.

Delphy, K. H. 1975. *Bau und Einrichtung von Gartenvolieren.* Philler-Verlag, Minden.

Deifenbach, K. 1979. Verhaltensbeobachtungen an Kakadus. *Die Voliere* 4, 147–152.

———. 1982. *Kakadus.* Müller-Verlag, Walsrode. [In English as *The World of Cockatoos,* T.F.H. Publications.]

Dilger, W. C. 1960. The comparative ethology of the African parrot-genus *Agapornis. Z. Tierpsychol.* 17, 648–685.

Ebert, U. 1978. *Vogelkrankheiten.* Schaper-Verlag, Hannover.

Forshaw, J. & W. Cooper. 1978. *Parrots of the World.* T.F.H. Publications, Neptune.

Fuhs, R. 1981. Geglückte Zucht eines Hellroten Aras. *AZ-Nachr.* H. 1, 14–15.

Gewalt, W. 1969. *Haltung und Zucht des Park- und Ziergeflügels.* Oertel & Spörer-Verlag, Reutlingen.

Grahl, W. de. 1974. *Papageien underer Erde,* Bd. II. Eigenverlag, Hamburg.

———. 1975. Erstzucht des Blaustirnzwergaras. *Gef. Welt,* H. 8, 141–143.

———. 1980. Zucht des Goldnackenaras bei K. Maass, Drensteinfurt. *AZ-Nachr.,* H. 1, 16.

Gregory, H. I. 1972. First breeding of the Green-winged Macaw in the United States. *Mag. Parrot Soc.,* 283–284.

Haas, G. 1977. Ara-Zuchten in Wuppertaler Zool. *AZ-Nachr.,* H. 4, 111-114.

Handschin, P. G. 1983. Seltener Zuchterfolg in Pfäffikon. *Gef. Freund,* H. 1, 18–19.

Haverschmidt, F. 1968. *Birds of Surinam.* Oliver & Boyd, London.

Hayward, J. 1983. Successful breeding of the Caninde Macaw in South Africa. *Cage & Aviary Birds,* Vol. 2.

Heeman, M. 1982. Geglückte Mischlingszucht zwischen Grünflügelara und Ararauna. *Gef. Welt,* H. 8, 239–240.

Heidenreich, M. 1980. Krankheiten der Papageienvögel. In Bielfeld, H. *Unzertrennliche—Agapornis.* Müller-Verlag, Walsrode. [In English as *Handbook of Lovebirds,* T.F.H. Publications.]

Hick, U. 1962. Beobachtungen über das Spielverhalten unserer Hyazintharas. *Freunde des Kölner Zoos* 5, 8–9.

Hill, A. 1981. Topographie der Vögel. *Orn. Mitt.* 34, H. 6, 133–138.

Hoppe, D. 1982. Zuchterfolge ohnegleichen beim Rotrückenara oder Maracana. *Gef. Welt,* H. 11, 347–348.

———. *Aras.* Ulmer, Stuttgart. [In English as *The World of Macaws,* T.F.H. Publications.]

Ingels, J., K. C. Parkes & J. Farrand. 1981. The status of the macaw generally but incorrectly called "Ara Caninde." *Le Gerfaut* 71, 283–294.

Ingram, K. A. 1982. Endoscopische Geschlectsbestimmung bei Papageien. *Gefl. Börse,* H. 21, 10.

Kemna, A. 1971. *Krankheiten der Stubenvögel.* Philler-Verlag, Minden.

Kirschofer, E. 1973. Zucht des Ararauna. *Gef. Welt,* H. 1, 1–3.

Krongerger, H. 1978. *Haltung von Vögeln—Krankheiten der Vögel.* Gustav Fischer-Verlag, Berlin & New York.

Lang, E. M. & R. Stamm. 1957. Zur Aufzucht eines Arabastardes im zool. Garten Basel. *Orn. Beob.* 54, 182–189.

Linn, H. 1978. Geglückte Zucht des Ararauna. *AZ-Nachr.*, H. 11, 372–374.

Low, R. 1980. *Parrots—Their Care and Breeding.* Blandford Press, Poole, Dorset.

———. Gelungene Zucht des Lear's Ara. *Gef. Freund,* H. 1, 18

Luther, D. 1970. *Die ausgestorbenen Vögel der Welt.* Ziemsen-Verlag, Wittenberg-Lutherstadt.

Meyer de Schauensee, R. 1970. *A Guide to the Birds of South America.* Livingston Publishing Company for the Academy of Natural Sciences of Philadelphia, Wynnewood.

Müller-Bierl, M. 1983. Bericht über Zuchtversuche und Aufzucht eines Hellroten Arara. *Die Voliere,* H. 3, 100–104.

O'Neill, J. P. 1969. Distributional notes on the birds of Peru, including twelve species previously unreported from the Republic. *Occ. Pap. Mus. Zool. La. St. Univ.* 37, 1-11.

Nilsson, G. & D. Mack. 1980. *Macaws: Traded to Extinction?* Traffic Special Report No. 2, Washington, D.C.

Peters, J. L. 1937. *Checklist of Birds of the World.* Harvard University Press, Cambridge.

Pinter, H. 1979. *Handbuch der Papageienkunde.* Franckh'sche Verlagshandlung, Stuttgart.

Ploog, H. 1982. Gelungene Zucht des Goldnackenaras. *Die Voliere,* H. 2, 58–59.

Raethel, H. S. 1968. *Krankheiten der Vögel.* Franck'sche Verlagshandlung, Stuttgart.

Reinhard, R. 1982. Caninde-Ara—Art oder Unterart? *Gef. Welt,* H. 4, 124–125.

Reynolds, M. W. 1977. Breeding the Grand Military Macaw at Bird Paradise, Cornwall. *Cage & Aviary Birds* 10, 13.

Ridgely, R. 1980. The current distribution and status of mainland neotropical parrots. In *Conservation of New World Parrots,* ICBP Techn. Publ. No. 1, St. Lucia.

Rigge, J. S. 1963. Breeding the Crimson or Green-winged Macaw. *Avic. Mag.* 69, 34–35.

Risdon, D. H. S. 1965. The breeding of the Blue and Yellow Macaw at the Tropical Bird Gardens, Rode. *Avic. Mag.* 71, 84–87.

Robiller, F. & K. Trogisch. 1982a. Wieder ein Paar Spix-Aras im Vogelpark Walsrode. *Die Voliere,* H. 6, 207–208.

———. 1982b. Ein Beitrag zum Verhalten des Hyazintharas. *Die Voliere,* H. 6, 207–208.

Rothschild, W. 1907. *Extinct Birds.* Hutchinson, London.

Ruß, K. 1882. *Sprechende Vögel,* Bd. I: *Die sprechenden Papageien.* Creuzsche Verlagshandlung, Magdeburg.

Schönwetter, M. 1964. *Handbuch der Oologie.* Akademie-Verlag, Berlin.

Sick, H. 1969. Aves Brasileiras ameacadas de extincao e noceos gerais de conservacao de aves no Brasil. *An. Acad. brasil. Cienc.* 41, 205–229.

———. 1979a. Decouverte de la patrie de l'Ara de Lear. *Alauda* 47 (1), 59–63.

———. 1979b. Die Herkunft von Lear's Ara entdeckt. *Gef. Welt,* H. 9, 161–162.

———. 1980. About the blue macaws, especially the Lear's Macaw. In *Conservation of New World Parrots,* Proc. ICBP Publ. No. 1., St. Lucia.

Sick, H. & D. M. Teixeira. 1980. Discovery of the home of the Indigo Macaw in Brasil. *American Birds,* Vol. 34, No. 2, 118–119, 212.

———. 1982–1983. Neue Vogelarten aus Brasilien und die Lösung des Rätsels der Blauen Araras. *Staden Jahrbuch, Beiträge zur Brasilkunde,* Bd. 30/31, Sao Paulo.

Simmons, K. E. L. 1957. The taxonomic significance of headscratching methods of birds. *Ibis* 99, 178–181.

Smith, G. A. 1971. The use of the foot in feeding, with especial reference to parrots. *Avic. Mag.* 77, 93-100.

Teitler, R. 1979. *Taming & Training Macaws.* T.F.H. Publications, Neptune.

Traylor, M. A. 1958. Birds of northeastern Peru. *Fieldiana, Zool.* 35, 87–141.

Vane, E. N. T. 1950. Noble Macaws. *Avic. Mag.* 56, 10–16.

Wennrich, G. 1983. Vögel als Spötter. *Die Voliere* 6, H. 2, 58–61.

Wetmore, A. 1968. *The birds of the republic of Panama.* Smithsonian Institution Press, Washington.

Wolters, H. E. 1975. *Die Vogelarten der Erde,* 1. Lief. Verlag Paul Parey, Hamburg.

Periodicals

Avicultural Magazine, Journal of the Avicultural Society, London.

AZ-Nachrichten, Munich.

Die Gefiederte Welt, Stuttgart.

Die Voliere, Hamburg.

Gefiederter Freund, Baar, Switzerland.

The Magazine of the Parrot Society, Bedford, England.

INDEX

Page numbers in **boldface** refer to illustrations.